Praise

'I loved this book, so much of it resonates with me and is an articulation of my own journey of data discovery over the years. This is not just a book for chief data officers and data management leads as it says in the intro, this is a handbook for any and all CXOs who have responsibility for or an interest in data – and that is ALL of them.'
— **Lorraine Waters**, Chief Data Officer, Global Compliance, HSBC and Top 100 Global Data Power Women 2020

'There has been a gold rush recently of CDO handbooks to feed the professional development of CDOs and aspiring CDOs. *Data Means Business* is THE handbook, not just for the senior data leaders, but the whole executive team who need to get with the data programme. Perhaps then, they can catch up with the new kids on the block, who have data as their heart and brain.'
— **Graeme McDermott**, Chief Data Officer, Tempcover

'Intelligent, witty and insightful. Barry and Jason eloquently discuss the challenging nature of business with the complexity of organisational culture to beautifully illustrate a framework to release value and create advantage from data that you may already hold. A must-read for all navigating the perilous economy of a post-COVID-19 world.'
— **Johanna Hutchinson**, Director of Data and Data Science, Joint Biosecurity Centre, Test and Trace, Dept of Health and Social Care; DataIQ Top 10 Most Influential People in Data 2021

'A must-read for finance leaders to learn the latest thinking around data in business.'
— **Patrick Marrinan**, Finance Director, Pho (Restaurant Group)

'*Data Means Business* takes the reader through a practical journey, arming executives with a toolkit and clear guidance on how to succeed with data. The book avoids jargon and provides a path to embracing what data can mean for individuals, their organisations and future transformation that could mean the different between failure, survival and prospering.'
— **Jagpal Jheeta**, CIO across multiple industries including retail, logistics and financial services

'When a caterpillar turns first into a larva and then into a butterfly, it has realised its destiny. When a business first "gets" data and then becomes data-guided, it can transform its own fortunes. With the frameworks in this book, you can accelerate that evolution and shorten the time between enabling yourself with data and creating value. To steal a phrase, this book gives you wings!'
— **David Reed**, Knowledge and Strategy Director, DataIQ

'The next time someone in your organization tells you that your data strategy can wait, just refer them to this book. It's a compelling read for those leaders seeking to truly unlock the value of data and evolve their organizations. *Data Means Business* converts the readers into data advocates.'
— **Gustavo Canton**, Analytics Leader, Starbucks

'Those businesses that ignore the value in data, or just pay it lip service, either won't be around for long or won't realise their ambitions. Many firms just don't know how to go about this and this book is aimed squarely at tackling that problem. *Data Means Business* really gets to the heart of this incredibly important topic, does so in a clear and jargon-free manner and shows how organisations can approach the change in a structured way that will deliver sustainable results. A must read!'
— **Darren Sharp**, Group IT Director, Tokio Marine Kiln

'Jason and Barry leverage the benefit of years of experience across hundreds of professional data engagements to draw up a framework anyone can use to harness and drive the advantages of data-guided decision making. This focused and easily digested book should be on the shelf of anyone leading a data transformation. Merging deep-sector expertise and the lessons from lean start-ups, they present their Level Up Framework that is easy-to-follow, easy-to-communicate and, hopefully, an easier route to driving business value from their data asset.'

— **Pete Williams**, Data Evangelist and Top 100 influencer in data

'Data, like money, is the most important asset of any organisation. Sadly, the data profession is a newborn compared to its grandparent – the finance profession. Organisations are waking up to the importance of data, but the immaturity of the data sector means only an elite few are able to really grasp the opportunities. With this influential book, Jason and Barry have created an anchor guide for the profession. The authors are levelling up the playing field with this practical guide for all leaders who understand they need to create data capability, but don't know what good looks like. Just read this and you will.'

— **Omid Shiraji**, Portfolio Chief Information Officer

'Only a few evangelist and internal entrepreneurs know how to marshal all the right resources across the right dimensions and in the right way. However, by using the ideas in this book we can start to make broader and real change.'

— **Devin Deen**, Associate Partner, Servian

'Data is the lifeblood of an organisation; like cashflow, without it your organisation won't survive, won't grow and won't flourish. Understanding your data, and the ecosystem it moves within, gives you an opportunity to drive differentiation and gain advantage on your savannah. In this book, Barry and Jason provide a simple and easily understood way to start understanding and using data better. A must-read for all senior leaders.'

— **Max Bailey**, Director, Lace Partners and ex Accenture Partner

'A great guide which I would highly recommend to all Chief Data Officers, future Heads of Data and business leaders to help them on their data journey. Unlike some guides which use technical jargon readily, *Data Means Business* instead offers simple steps to deliver an effective data-led organisation.'

— **Katie Hevey**, Digital & Data Practice Leader, Leathwaite

Data Means Business

Level up your organisation to adapt, evolve and scale in an ever-changing world

Jason Foster and Barry Green

Rᵉthink

Contents

Foreword

Most of us would say we know a thing or two about data: its purpose, its value, its place in the universe. Today it's everywhere – on smartphones, social media, TV, advertising and even that annoying voice on your GPS nagging at you to turn left or right. At that level, it's very familiar to us. We depend upon it continually and exchange it regularly. We communicate, coordinate and control using it. It literally glues our world together.

We regard it with intimacy and reverence, but do we understand it? Few have bothered to even consider that question. It's a sobering thought that many of today's seminal decisions are made in the presence of such a void.

We have a word for these decisions, a word itself often treated with reverence and misunderstanding. That word is 'strategy', and a quick flick through the dictionary gives its definition as:

Strategy: *noun*
/ strǽtədʒi /
(pl. strategies)

1. [countable] a plan that is intended to achieve a particular purpose
   - *the government's economic strategy*
   - strategy for doing something *to develop a strategy for dealing with unemployment*
   - strategy to do something *It's all part of an overall strategy to gain promotion.*

2. [uncountable] the process of planning something or putting a plan into operation in a skillful way
   - *marketing strategy*

3. [uncountable, countable] the skill of planning the movements of armies in a battle or war; an example of doing this
   - *military strategy*
   - *defence strategies*[1]

In my role as a technical leader, I've met many decision-makers who lack even the faintest grasp of either data or strategy yet still they hold the reins of many

---

1   Definition of 'strategy', Oxford Learner's Dictionary, www. oxfordlearnersdictionaries.com / definition / american_english / strategy

household companies. I've shared time with them, both formally and informally, over many meetings, lunches and chats beside coin-operated vending machines. All in the hope they might stand back, just for a moment, and consider their data in the wider context that is the global network of exchange around us.

The message is simple: data is about more than economics and business, technology and influence. Today data is key not only to the individual, but is vital across every Ma and Pa outfit, through the largest corporates and on to the governments that control every aspect of our lives. We also have a word for that, but most dictionaries haven't caught up yet.

That word is 'sociotechnical' and it describes how data now pervades every aspect of the human condition. I use this word increasingly often, but before I bring it out I mentally prepare, hoping eyebrows will raise in the boardroom but telling myself to expect the conversation to move on swiftly. To be asked to return to the agenda. That's how I first met Barry Green, the chief data officer at a large financial services organisation. I remember the day well. On that day I was cut short mid-segue.

'What was that? What did you say...?' I remember Barry saying. Clear, concise, interested.

'Stop. You've just said something important...'

What ensued was a deeply relevant and insightful conversation. Barry had already taken time out to think about data properly, but he knew that his understanding was incomplete.

Jason Foster brings with him a background that complements Barry's. He's advised large-scale enterprise in ways that transcend the limits of traditional business, and which deliberately embrace both the digital and social. Like Barry, his time at the top has given him real insight into what works, while still appreciating that things could be done differently.

But how? The 'how' is in this book.

Barry's and Jason's record speaks for itself. Between them they have crafted the data strategy of some of the world's most prestigious companies and, more than that, have helped to implement their guidance with credibility and skill – a rare feat in industry.

More than that, they understand how modern technology has changed the world and what that means for business. They get that data is at the very heart of that change and how it affects every aspect of commerce, organisation and society. In doing that, in their hands, data literally comes to life to explain its position in the evolving network of ecosystems that is modern business. In that, I applaud them.

This is essential reading for all executives who understand that there is value in their data and want to extract as much of that value as possible. It's a signpost to a brave new world that most established businesses still choose to ignore but cannot avoid. This is data strategy for the twenty-first century.

I'll leave it up to Barry and Jason to explain.

Professor Philip Tetlow PhD
Author, TED Speaker, CEO and CTO

Introduction

In nature everything is interdependent; there are millions of small ecosystems existing together. When they are all connected, they make up our environment. Small changes in an ecosystem can have big impacts on the immediate and overall environment. Plankton disappearing from the sea or honeybee numbers reducing will have effects disproportionate to their overall physical size. These ecosystems are fragile and unexpected change can have catastrophic consequences. It is important to understand and manage our understanding of these interdependencies. By learning and developing our understanding we can continue to enjoy the environment in which we live, even as it evolves.

Darwin's theory of evolution by natural selection provides a way to understand the interdependencies but also how and why the overall environment has evolved. Evolution is continuous. Business is another example of an ecosystem. Millions of businesses exist in different countries, creating different services and products, seemingly independent of each other. As an ecosystem each business has a set of components, living (people) and nonliving (systems), and while it exists for a specific purpose the dependencies on the overall environment are there.

It is our responsibility as leaders to drive change and manage business not just for profit but for employees, shareholders, society and the environment. Like the environment, the business ecosystem is changing at a rapid pace. Power in society and the way consumers engage with brands is shifting. Our choice for services has continued to explode. Big technology players are gobbling up market demand and killing off long-established brands. Like evolution, change is continuous.

If we try to manage this change by focusing on only one aspect of the business ecosystem, we are bound to fail. COVID-19 has highlighted the fragilities of industries, economies and governments and shown that we are connected, perhaps more than we realised. The ability to adapt in a world where we may need to 'lock down' cities, regions or countries without destroying the social and economic fabric means digital enablement is key to protecting our businesses and the broader environment. A digital environment is becoming critical for us to maintain business ecosystems. It is also a natural evolution. An unseen virus is forcing us to innovate and evolve but it must be done in an ethical and sustainable way.

As leaders we need to do things differently to bring about change. We cannot keep doing the same things in the same ways and expecting different results. We need to digitise the way we operate, implement faster and connect things in an ethical and responsible way to be better prepared for systemic changes to our environment. But being digital is not as simple as people, process and technology.

Data – electronic information stored in systems – is a key component that needs to be better connected, understood, managed and used for the evolution of business. To build a new ecosystem we need to digitise the inputs and address all components. Key dependencies are process, people and culture. Process gives data context. People interact through process to create data. Data, people and process are influenced by the culture in which data is created. We need to look at data as a social science, not only through a technology or data lens. Data will be a conduit to highlighting why we need to change. Technology will be needed to ensure we reuse, maintain and manage data. But this should not be where we start.

Culture in society and in the broader business context is also changing. Advances in technology are opening up potential for enterprise, society and individuals. With that, data is fast becoming the lifeblood of successful organisations, both for profit and not for profit. Those that can capture, manage, analyse and make data an enabler for transformation have an opportunity to move ahead. Some of this change is positive: collaborative working and the power of utilising difference. But this evolution is slow and legacy thinking is still prevalent. We need to change the narrative. The legacy issues – silos, obsolete organisational culture, lack of agility – will persist unless we change the approach. Are you ready to change?

The business environment has millions of ecosystems and your own organisation is one ecosystem created to solve a specific problem. The data evolution is needed to ensure we maximise value and create an environment that works in a complex and fast-moving world. Those who do not adjust to changes in cultural norms and ways of working, thinking and adopting technology in a positive way risk falling behind or becoming obsolete. The stark reality is that things need to change. Wrapping our heads around what we in business need to do to get ahead is critical to a sustainable and scalable future business.

We need to manage cultural and behavioural change. We need to move fast, create simplicity and be pragmatic. There is no silver bullet. By using a holistic approach based around adaptable ideas, we will walk you through how you can lead change, connecting all the dependencies. We also adopt a start-up approach to making data an enabler in an age when digital adoption is necessary for business and society to evolve.

Are you ready to evolve? Because data means business.

The primary purpose of this book is to create momentum around thinking about data differently. It is not meant as a step-by-step guide. We provide approaches that have been successfully deployed, along with fundamental tools, methods and ideas. If you are ready to create change in your organisation, this book will help frame your thinking and put you on the path to success.

It will show how to create the right method for your organisation and ensure you have a clear alignment of the business strategy to your data strategy. It favours pragmatism over perfection, collaboration and cooperation over siloed thinking and business, and new ways of working over outdated data strategies and initiatives.

This book is for business leaders wanting to understand the best approaches to get value from data before you embark and for those looking to accelerate a journey they are already on. It will help you to understand data's context within an organisation's ecosystem and how to create a culture of learning; it promotes insight-guided decision-making and will help you keep your data strategy focused not on data but on your business. This book will help you level up your organisation so it can adapt, evolve and scale.

This book is for chief data officers and other data leaders looking to build their strategy and get early, continual and sustained success. It will provide clear guidance on what to think about and how to start, scale and get the best results out of your data strategy for your business. Show it to your peers, leadership team and board so they 'get' what you are trying to achieve and how.

Finally, this book is for aspiring data leaders wanting to learn the breadth of challenge and opportunities required to be successful and who are ready to step up into that leadership position. It will help you level up your knowledge, business acumen, commercial awareness, leadership prowess and understanding of how your current role is fundamental to the success of your organisation.

This book is designed for you to dip into the relevant topics when you need to. Keep coming back to it to remind you of the tools and approaches. Use it to explain to others what you are trying to achieve and how. There are sections that frame mindset and concepts and others that walk through the journey you will need to go on, so you may also get value from working through each stage to make sure you haven't missed anything.

Part 1: Thinking Differently helps to frame some of the key concepts, lessons and mindsets required to be successful in modern business and in an innovative, progressive data strategy. We also introduce the Level Up Framework, which shapes the stages discussed in Parts 2 and 3.

Part 2: Getting Off The Ground focuses on the early stages of your data journey and helps put organisation-wide roots down in a way that assures success. It explains how to create momentum, get the organisation behind the journey and build credibility.

Part 3: Growth And Impact helps you move out of thinking, planning and proofs of concept to scale at pace and create an organisation guided by data. There are stories from some great organisations that have achieved success by applying data to everything they do.

Part 4: Defining And Delivering Your Strategy brings everything together to explain how to assess where you are and how to plan, build a data strategy and monitor progress.

PART 1

THINKING DIFFERENTLY

The ability of an organisation to not only survive but thrive through good and challenging times is predicated on its ability to listen, learn and adapt; to build a culture that can not only handle change but has a thirst for it. Organisations that stand still run the risk of becoming obsolete. It may not happen overnight but the world around you will chip away and eventually the inevitable will happen.

Once, Blockbuster was flying high; at its peak it had 9,000 stores globally and $5.9 billion in revenue, but the company missed the opportunity that online DVD rentals and then streaming presented to the industry. The technology changed and their customers changed how they wanted to consume content. Blockbuster didn't pivot and missed the chance to continue to own the home movie consumption market. Enter Netflix and multiple other streaming services: Rakuten, Disney+, Prime Video... In 2000, Blockbuster turned down the opportunity to acquire Netflix for $50m and with it the future in home entertainment. Once a darling on the high street, Blockbuster is now out of business.[2]

2   F Olito, 'The rise and fall of Blockbuster', *Business Insider*, 20 August 2020, www.businessinsider.com/rise-and-fall-of-blockbuster

The change imperative is real. This section shares ways to think about your business in the context of your data strategy. It looks at business as an ecosystem and lessons we can learn from start-ups in how they test, evolve and iterate their value proposition. We explore people science and culture change as fundamental enablers. We consider the importance of ethics and diversity in your strategy. We introduce the idea of data as a product, data as a service and the Level Up Framework.

ONE

A New Approach

The business ecosystem

On the African savannah there are thousands of life forms coexisting that are completely dependent on each other. Somehow, a correct balance is maintained. Water, air and grass are fundamental to the balance. Animal populations are estimated to have reduced by 70% in the last fifty years.[3] It is estimated that 99.9% of

---

3   A Kelley, 'Human activity has wiped out nearly 70 percent of the world's wildlife in just 50 years: report', Changing America, 10 September 2020, https://thehill.com/changing-america/sustainability/environment/515808-human-activity-has-wiped-out-nearly-70-percent-of

all species that have ever lived are extinct.[4] What does this have to do with data?

Despite all the hype, data is still not managed and used effectively. Without it an organisation could not survive, but like air it is taken for granted and assumed to be there. It is created in our processes, captured, digitised and may or may not be made available for decision-making. Given the increasing understanding that data is a fundamental part of an organisation, we need to change how we think about it, not just in our organisation but in the wider business, economic and social environment.

People, process and technology have become people, process, technology and data. But this simple addition of data to an established change approach is not sufficient. Business is infinitely more complex. People are intricate and in our organisations we have created silos. We categorise and label behaviour, diversity, jobs and organisational structures, making the ecosystem hard to navigate. Culture is not something you can touch, yet it is an important part of getting an organisation to be data-guided. Using and managing data effectively is complex. Like the savannah, the business ecosystem is reliant on more than just the obvious factors.

---

4   C Wilcox, 'Human-caused extinctions have set mammals back millions of years', *National Geographic*, 17 October 2018, www.nationalgeographic.com/animals/2018/10/millions-of-years-mammal-evolution-lost-news

Gartner have defined eight variables for a business ecosystem: strategy, openness, participants, relationships, value exchange, industries, complexity and technology.[5] James F Moore coined the term 'business ecosystem', which he described as a setting in which 'companies co-evolve capabilities around a new innovation: they work cooperatively and competitively to support new products, satisfy customer needs and eventually incorporate the next round of innovations'.[6] Thinking about business like an ecosystem is intended to drive innovation, growth and a more effective business.

This is only one version of what a business ecosystem is, but it demonstrates that if we are to implement the change needed to become a data-guided organisation we need to move away from thinking about data as special and separate. When implementing data, we need to use it to connect the organisation. Data governance has traditionally been about a 'command and control' model. Data is not just governance, it has an ecosystem that exists in your organisation and the broader social and economic ecosystems. We will help you gauge when to implement data change into your organisation. We provide the tools and ideas to help

5   K Panetta, '8 dimensions of business ecosystems', Gartner, 12 July 2017, www.gartner.com/smarterwithgartner/8-dimensions-of-business-ecosystems

6   J Moore, 'Predators and prey: A new ecology of competition', *Harvard Business Review*, 1999, 71(3): 75–86, https://hbr.org/1993/05/predators-and-prey-a-new-ecology-of-competition

get you thinking differently about data so that you can evolve and not become extinct.

Data means business, business means data

Making and executing decisions is the bread and butter of business leaders, operators and workers across the world.

Where to deploy resources? How should we invest our money? What should I offer this customer who is about to leave us? How do I get charitable donations from more members? Who are our customers and how do I retain them? How do I maximise capital? What are the chances of success in our targeted regions? How do we balance adding value to the shareholders, employees and society? Every day, decisions to be made that have huge consequences.

To help answer these questions, make decisions and deliver results, organisations create a vision, set their strategy and allocate money and resources to implementing day-to-day operations, changes and strategic objectives. They get their teams behind that strategy, execute it and then try to track how they are performing. In the best case everything is successful; in the worst case we fail as a business. The business environment is becoming increasingly complex with supply chain vulnerability, geo-political risk and variable availability of capital and skills.

Heraclitus, a Greek philosopher, argued that change is the only constant.[7] We add to that: 'Uncertainty is the only thing we're certain of.' We cannot plan for or know what's coming all the time. We can only set ourselves up to deal with that uncertainty and be able to respond. In his book *Management: Tasks, responsibilities, practices*, Peter Drucker argued that strategic planning and innovation should be carried out on the basis that the future is uncertain and unpredictable.[8] Since we cannot predict what will happen, it's about getting better at taking the right risks rather than removing them completely. We need to embrace change, embrace uncertainty and set ourselves up accordingly.

Our basic human need is to feel like we belong, that we are part of something special and exciting. Increasingly this means fair pay for our work and a recognition that what we do has value to our customers and society. We are looking for a trend of positive outcomes: more successes than failures, more upsides than downsides, more predictability in outcomes than shooting in the dark, and better management through uncertain, changing times.

---

7   Stanford Encyclopedia of Philosophy, 'Heraclitus', 3 September 2019, https://plato.stanford.edu/entries/heraclitus

8   P Drucker, *Management: Tasks, responsibilities, practices* (Taylor & Francis, 1973)

Data is the enabler that will help us achieve this outcome. That's it. It's about helping to plan better, react faster, manage through ambiguity, listen and learn concisely, get more consistency, make decisions consciously and thoughtfully. It's about better understanding your failures and your successes and applying that learning to get better next time. If you can do all these things, you win, but winning requires a consistent approach to solving the root problem.

Data is a business skill. A big, critical, value-adding, differentiating skill. Like understanding budgets, managing people, procuring products and services and engaging with partners, the skill of data is something that you and your team must develop for getting and staying ahead. Data is a business profession. The industry tends to use the phrase 'data literacy' and this is essentially what it means – an organisation that is able to apply insights to a business situation in order to make better decisions. Getting value out of data is therefore everyone's responsibility. Data means business.

Pete Williams, a data evangelist who has held senior leadership positions in brands including Penguin Random House, Marks & Spencer and John Lewis, says:

'Everyone in an organisation uses data to make a decision. They may not refer to it as such, you'll need to help them with that realisation. But they do. What they don't usually know is what data is available that may help them to a faster, better decision, or how to ask a different question that might yield a better answer.'[9]

Creating the data-guided business

It's important to create a business that has data at the centre of all decision-making. Decision-making on strategy development, operational execution, reaction to internal or external events and engaging with your stakeholders. It won't make the decisions for you but leads to a combination of human smarts, intuition and leadership guided by the insights and learning that data gives us.

The evolution of where and how data is maximised in your business fundamentally shifts the return you get from the investments in using data. Your use of data and how pervasive it is, in decision-making specifically, determines how data-guided you can be. The diagram below shows the states you can be in with regard to the pervasiveness of data for decision-making.

---

9   Interview with Pete Williams, 23 November 2020

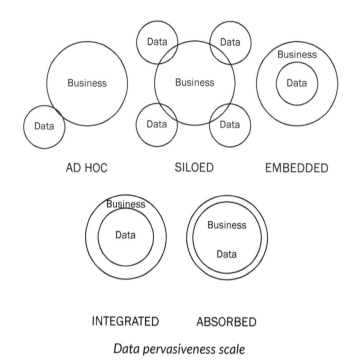

Data pervasiveness scale

Since data is an enabler and a conduit for connecting the organisation, you want to move away from a place where data is not used by the business to drive the agenda. It should not be seen as separate, outside the day job and for someone else to deal with. It should not be ad hoc and held or managed in silos. It needs to move to a place where the use, activation and change made through data should be pervasive and seamless with the job of your teams. It is about being embedded, integrated and absorbed into how you operate.

COVID-19 has shown that the ability to adapt is key for survival. Even if you want to be a 100% digital business you still need to operate in an ecosystem where not everything can be done digitally.

If you want to be a data-guided business, you will need to know what data is needed, create processes to digitise inputs and understand what and how you operate, think, behave and what impact the external ecosystem has on your organisation.

Data-guided and digitally savvy businesses exist but they are not the norm. There are organisations that use data effectively and some are 100% digital. But are they fully optimised? Can they explain and measure how things are done? Do they use this to continually evolve? These businesses are the exception, not the rule. Think of Netflix, Facebook, Uber. Think of online marketplaces like Amazon, ASOS and Alibaba. They are data and digital native. They have grown up striving for and succeeding in having data absorbed into their operations, processes and decision-making.

Many organisations continue to operate in a manner that does not adopt digital and data effectiveness, though, generally because of the legacy that has been created but also because of old mindsets and inertia. Data is still not embraced, embedded and integrated due to the large amount of change needed. Change is hard.

The lucky few that get to a point where data is absorbed into the fabric of the business can state they are a data-guided organisation and can act like the digital and data natives of this world. They will see the incremental benefit that operating in this way has and gain considerable competitive advantage over others. But they need to continue to evolve and be set up to do this effectively.

The data value chain

What do we mean by data? Ask a room full of people what data is and you will get a different answer from everyone. Some will talk about a report they get, some will talk about the attributes captured in a CRM (customer relationship management) database, some will talk about the output of an algorithm, some will say it's what Facebook collects, some may even say it's something they get with their phone contract so they can watch Netflix and TikTok videos.

Data ambiguity creates a challenge in terms of understanding what problem we are solving. Getting the most value from data requires us to understand it at all stages of its lifecycle and value chain. How many times have you heard that data is out of scope for a project? How many times have you heard the term 'data' used in multiple different contexts in a meeting? How many times have you heard: 'Why don't we have the data we need?'

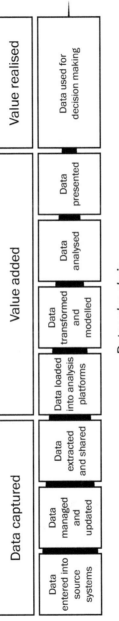

Data captured		Value added				Value realised
Data entered into source systems	Data managed and updated	Data extracted and shared	Data loaded into analysis platforms	Data transformed and modelled	Data analysed	Data presented	Data used for decision making

Data value chain

The answer is that data can mean different things to different people depending on the stage of the data value chain they are referring to, often without them knowing. The diagram above shows this value chain and why different interpretations exist.

1. Data is captured (eg a website sign-up form creating a new record in your CRM system or creation of a new product in your product management system), data is managed in that source system (eg customer records are enhanced with new attributes, financial transactions are adjusted, notes are added to records) and then data is extracted from those source systems (eg moving customer data from the CRM system into your email campaign engine) or taken out for the purposes of adding value.

2. Data has value added to it – it can be uploaded to a data and analytics platform, transformed through aggregation, consolidation, calculation, manipulation, then analysed to find insights, answers, trends and patterns. It will be presented to a human for interpretation or a system for further use and processing.

3. The value of the data is realised – the use of the data should drive an action (eg changing an email campaign, fixing a broken process, launching a new product) that aims to change outcomes and realise value.

At all these stages data is classed as 'the data' so it's important to recognise the different lenses and increasing value that data has as it passes through this value chain.

A start-up philosophy

This is not another trendy metaphor. This is a philosophy we suggest you adopt to help facilitate the change needed to embed data into the DNA of your organisation. There is a lot to learn from the mindset used in successful start-ups that move out of those early stages and grow exponentially for incredible results.

Let's start by describing some key attributes of a start-up that we can use in developing a data function:

- They have an idea that is new and innovative.

- They aim to solve a problem when there is no obvious alternative.

- Success is not guaranteed and requires entrepreneurial thinking and leadership.

- In the early stages, a start-up is small and has not yet developed a scalable product or service.

- Start-ups use speed and design as a key differentiator. They are not constrained by the 'as is' or 'legacy'.

- They use an approach that lets them test an idea, learn from it and scale the things that are working.

- They build an early version of their product or service, often called a minimum viable product (MVP), which has the minimum required to add value and test the proposition.

- They do not have long-term funding and need to prove value to get funding, survive and thrive.

- Start-ups are drivers of change.

There are plenty of excellent books on the subject of start-ups. Eric Ries' *The Start-Up Way* is a good example if you want to learn more about how to apply the start-up mentality and approach in organisations more generally.[10]

We are not saying your organisation should actually be a start-up. The philosophy is important, though. It's about adaptability, pragmatism, testing and learning, listening and reacting appropriately. Often in organisations the culture stymies employees in acting differently. Our approach is based around treating data like a new product or service and bringing that to market in the organisation.

---

10 E Ries, *The Start-Up Way: How entrepreneurial management transforms culture and drives growth* (Portfolio, 2017)

Data is prevalent in everything your organisation does. The issue of how to manage data and bring value is a holistic issue. Adopting this approach in your data function allows you to change the culture from the inside with real behaviours and ensure you show progress in a progressive, positive way. You can use this approach regardless of the maturity of your data function. This is fundamentally about changing how you look at and use data. This means being innovative, thinking differently and solving problems pragmatically.

Organisations often start with a data governance-focused function to 'sort out data'. Like any ecosystem, your data function needs to have several components to provide real value. Apply the start-up approach to this fundamental question: where do I start with data?

Let's look at this through a business lens. Most organisations are looking to digitise how they operate. It's fundamental to understand how the process needs to change, what data is needed to achieve a series of business outcomes and what technologies are needed to support this change. Will data governance solve this problem? No. So what data components do we need?

- Understand the 'as-is' business process.

- Understand the data flow through the process.

- Define what data means. This ensures there is a consistent understanding of the attributes and metrics used.

- Ensure the information produced in the process and to support the process is robust and can be trusted.

- Understand the links between process, data, people, risk and opportunity.

These factors form the basis of our MVP. We break down what is needed and don't assume 'data governance' is the answer. By defining what we need from data we are effectively creating a list of data solutions and activities we may need. This list will grow as you mature but you need a starting point. You can also use this list to understand if any of the services or products exist in any part of your organisation and can act as a catalyst. Now we have defined a set of things we need – what next? We need to set a plan and move at pace.

You may have heard the term 'fail fast' – we don't like this. In many organisations there is a culture of failure being bad and in a political environment this can be detrimental. The start-up philosophy we use stresses 'test and learn'. Everything you undertake has some learning value, no matter how small. In an organisation we have worked with, we ran a number of MVPs on the existing data management tooling to see if we could connect all the data components needed for us to adopt a consistent data management approach (process, business glossary, metadata etc). The outcome was clear: no. However, the team learned why they needed to connect the various data components, they learned more about what they needed from new tools and they started thinking differently about data.

By running small, fast MVP activities, you can use the output to shape the next set of actions and have a story to tell about why you are moving in a certain direction. There is a need for pace and results. By adopting a test and learn approach we develop a 'good enough' rather than 'perfect' solution, knowing it will be improved to meet future business needs as we scale.

The process is not optimal and there are some quick wins on improving the process. People involved in the process understand there is not a common understanding of key terms in the business, and you may find a data attribute in a metric is not representative of the meaning understood by the business. If we take a start-up approach, we look to develop an MVP that allows us to take the next decision. We use the outputs from our MVP as a learning exercise, hence the term test and learn.

In the example above we also ran workshops with the broader set of stakeholders to get a picture of the issues in our data journey. We then defined several different MVPs to look at tools and started to bring together a plan for developing the necessary data services to ensure we could meet current and future business objectives. The output of this session helped shape a common understanding of what and why we needed to move forward with certain MVPs over others and helped to align the thinking of the team. It showed why operating differently was needed and started to embed a different culture in the data team.

Culture and the science of people

Culture, like the broader business ecosystem, is not static and evolves through a collective set of beliefs, values and attitudes. Culture has an impact on the strategic direction of the business and influences management decisions in all business functions. However, it is often not considered when looking at data. Changing how we understand, manage and use data will influence the beliefs, values and attitudes of the organisation. Data leadership is a conduit for change, linking technology, business and all silos in an organisation. No matter what the existing culture is in an organisation, if you need to improve your use of data you will need to change culture. The start-up philosophy is one way to start that change.

Much is written about creating a data-driven culture, or as we prefer to call it a data-guided culture. The focus is then often on data. How data is used, who uses it, what it's for. We train people in data and recruit new data people in the hope that the culture will change. This misses the point. For an organisation to be guided by data and maximise the opportunities it presents, we need to understand the culture and values of the business itself and marry those with the key cultural values needed to be a data-guided organisation.

When a start-up organisation begins it is small and can make decisions fast. Test and learn at pace is all about getting the product/service to the next phase of development. Everything you do should have value. By collaborating and working outside organisational norms, you will be influencing beliefs and attitudes. We have often heard the statement: 'That won't work in our business.' You will need to be resilient. You can't start by trying to change the entire business culture, but you can influence how the data team behaves and interacts with the broader business. You are trying to change from within by starting small and then finding new ways to 'go viral'. You are looking for three key outcomes:

1. Ensure you make progress and can show success.

2. Be an incubator for doing things differently and slowly influence the 'old' culture of the organisation.

3. By establishing the need for products and services, you can change the narrative for data.

If you have an established team or no team, if you are an old conservative organisation or even a start-up, it is likely there will be a need to change. This philosophy works for any organisation. It is fundamentally about creating that conduit for change. Communication, collaboration, pragmatism, test and learn, pace and connecting the components of the organisation's ecosystems all allow data-guided thinking.

Culture is organisation-wide but within the organisation there are often subcultures. This helps create the silos that exist. This culture is often used as an excuse for inefficiency. How often have you heard someone say: 'That's just the way we do it here'? It's logical that when thinking about data strategy we should start thinking about the business outcomes and the people needed to achieve results. Process defines the ways of working and is a point of reference for what is important and where to start. There is a danger in many organisations of starting not with understanding culture but implementing the next sexy thing.

The thinking and ways of working brought into a business (and therefore the culture) are impacted heavily by the data industry itself, often detrimentally. The industry is awash with discussion, news, research, articles and focus on artificial intelligence, deep learning, data science, statistics, predictions and algorithms. This is a world of science – a world where analytical and mathematical algorithms like linear regression, multivariate adaptive regression splines, neural networks and k-nearest neighbours are pointed at data and set to work.

This has led many to make data science the heart of at least their thinking, if not their doing. A world where facts and maths are used to infer, to learn, to devise probabilities and make predictions to offer us the right outfit, the right songs, recommend the right hospital treatment, deliver us the best advert, assess us for insurance risk and make ordering from Amazon even easier than it is now. The science of data is king – right?

When you are told AI is the next 'silver bullet' for your organisational problems, you need to take a step back. There is no silver bullet. Algorithms need data to learn. Creating algorithms that are not operationally effective, no matter how clever, will not bring true value. Data science is one of many components needed to maximise your understanding of what and how you operate. They can help simplify and auto-mate decisions but they need to exist in processes that touch real people and be managed and move with change in both the internal organisation and the external environment.

In this world of maths and data science, it is the science of people and the art of understanding and getting the best from people that really impact the outcomes for most organisations. That's culture.

Data science or people science? Data is as much about culture and your people as it is about process technology and other factors that influence the overall business ecosystem. Harnessing the science of people will help you drive your business forward and create an organisation guided by data.

Thinking about ethics and diversity

Two key components of driving change in business and society are (1) better ethical decisions and (2) the ability to celebrate, understand and use the differences between people.

Why be ethical? Nowadays environment transparency and visibility are only a click away. Acting unethically and not being noticed is unlikely. The most visible example of this is Facebook and the use of its data by Cambridge Analytica. This revelation had an instant impact on the company's share price and has continued to influence the direction of Facebook.[11] While the damage to the share price can be temporary, the reputational damage generally has a much longer tail.

There are numerous examples in the past of businesses acting in an unethical manner. In the 1940s

---

11 J White, 'Facebook stock value plunges amid Cambridge Analytica controversy', *The Independent*, 19 March 2018, www.independent.co.uk/news/business/news/facebook-stock-market-value-cambridge-analytica-data-breach-a8264251.html

and 1950s, cigarettes were marketed as good for your health. Companies even used doctors to reinforce the message in advertising. The cigarette industry at some point realised that this was not true.[12] Despite knowing the health impacts, they continued to market cigarettes as safe. Did you get into business to harm the environment, individuals or your employees? How you react to new information can be the difference between acting ethically or unethically.

How you embed ethical behaviour in your organisation is part of your culture. If it is not explicit, there will be an implicit cultural norm. Given the increased use of AI and decisions being made by algorithms, ethics hype in data is on the rise. People are concerned about how we use data. This is positive and necessary. But ethics is not just a data issue. Ethics and how you make decisions should be consistent in all parts of the organisation. Your understanding of the culture around ethics needs to be considered. If the consistency is low then, like all things in business, you can use data as an enabler to help change the culture and process.

Diversity, like ethics, has an increasing focus in society and therefore in our organisations. In simple terms, diversity is about understanding and utilising the different experiences we have that shape us as indi-

---

12 M Gardner and AM Brandt, 'The doctor's choice is America's choice', *Am J Public Health*, 2006, 96(2): 222–232, www.ncbi.nlm.nih. gov/pmc/articles/PMC1470496

viduals. By having varying viewpoints on problems you can ensure that input in your organisation is not one-dimensional. However, diversity is a lot more complex than skin colour or sexual orientation.

To effect change you need to have an organisation that embraces difference and uses these differences to effectively solve problems. Managing diversity is not easy but there are benefits for the organisation; it forces change and provides an opportunity for people to evaluate their previous bias. Take the example of hiring people in your data function with autism. High-functioning autism may require us to change the working environment and the way we manage people. How we instruct people and the work itself will need to be thought through to ensure we have happy and productive employees.

Diversity is about being able to manage and understand difference to drive real change. Like ethics, diversity needs a holistic approach and needs to be consistent. The diversity wheel below highlights the complexity and the bias that can and does exist. As individuals we are not one-dimensional; like an ecosystem we have multiple inputs that make us who we are.

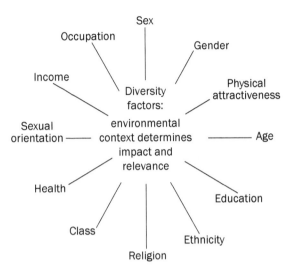

Human diversity characteristics

Regardless of any regulation, it makes sense to change the way we drive more ethical behaviour, use data and understand why the differences between us can make both business and broader society a better place. Profit is still fundamental. However, a better balance is needed to drive holistic value and create more flexible organisations as society and business evolve.

Data products and services

The benefit of thinking about data as a product or service is that it forces the user to answer the questions: what do I want to do with the data? What is the outcome and what is involved in getting my need solved?

The problem with the term 'data' is that it has multiple meanings depending on context. The concept of data products and services has been around for a while but it is difficult to implement unless you have a holistic approach to making data an enabler. 'I can't get the data I need' can mean an issue with access to a system, the data may not be available, or the data is not well defined and therefore is not available. 'The data is wrong' could mean that the filters used to produce the report have led to an unexpected outcome, or the answer interpreted from the data is not what the user wants to hear. 'The data quality is poor' could mean the source of the data is incomplete, or that the meaning of the data is not consistent and understood. 'I need the data' could mean an excel data dump, a report or data available in a data warehouse. Instead of talking about data, we must change the narrative to understand what we need to do with data to meet a business outcome.

The business needs to become data-guided. To achieve this, everyone should be able to communicate what they need from data. You don't do this by talking about 'data'; you do it by ensuring everyone can use data effectively in whatever role they have in the organisation. To do this we will define what users need from data with a set of products and services. This allows users to clearly understand what they need from the data and will help the data literacy improve over time. The products and services concept is the method we will use to change the narrative and deliver results with pace.

Data as a product

As citizens and consumers, we interact with products and services all the time. These can be digital products like Spotify and Netflix; physical products like bread, televisions, shoes; or hybrid products that blend physical and digital such as Amazon or Uber where you engage with a digital product (an app in this instance) to get access to a physical product or service.

Products usually exist to solve a customer need. You want to listen to music or watch a movie, you are hungry so you need some food or you're going for a run so need a pair of trainers. The product has been created to satisfy that need. Each product will have many features including its cost, its uses, where it can be stored, how long it lasts, the sizes it comes in, the people you can share it with and so on depending on the product. Individual products can also be used as part of another product and the value of the finished good is greater than the value of any of the individual ingredients.

The company that provides that product will have metrics (or key performance indicators, KPIs) to assess the performance of that product – number of products sold, monthly active users, monthly recurring revenue, stock holding, profitability, units in transit, customer satisfaction score, value of wastage and so on. These metrics tell the company how that product is performing and should guide it towards how to improve the performance or whether it is time to retire it in favour of new and better products.

Each of the products generated or services provided by the company will be owned by someone. They act as the manager for that product and are measured on its success. While different industries have different names for this, they are essentially the product manager. In digital teams this is a common role and is usually broken down into components of the overall product. For example, at Spotify there may be a different product manager for the 'Discover Weekly' product than there will be for the 'Sign Up' product.

There are proven benefits of treating data as a product in your organisation in a similar way to physical and digital products. You will see in the figure below a comparison between the products used to create a smoothie (finished good) and the products used to create a data product, for example a dashboard, a recommendation engine or an algorithm (finished goods), to show how the concept of a consumer product can be applied to a data product.

These are all examples of data products that you could build to support business outcomes:

- Transaction enrichment product
- Customer service bot

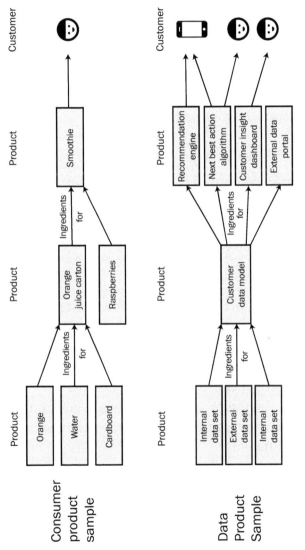

Consumer product vs data as a product example

- Manual process automation

- Sales dashboard

- Pricing optimisation engine

- Predictive model

- Data extraction process

- Recommendation engine

Some of these data products are there to serve as ingredients for other products and some are finished goods in their own right. Like the consumer products mentioned, each data product:

- Exists to solve a customer need

- Has features and KPIs

- Has a product manager who owns the features and is measured on the KPIs

While each data product may be in the same technology ecosystem, the underlying technology used to create the product may be different. For example, the technology you use to create a sales dashboard will be different to the technology you use to build a predictive model. Each data product can have one or many uses and ways of people and systems accessing said product. A recommendation engine might be accessed by its output being served up to a website so the customer sees personalised products in real time. It may also provide an output that creates relevant recommendations in an outbound email campaign. This is just like the smoothie in the example. That smoothie could be bought from a shop, a kiosk, a vending machine or in a restaurant.

Chief data officer at Aramisauto in France, Anne-Claire Baschet, says:

> 'Often the main priority for data leaders is focused around adoption. This is predicated on building something like a data warehouse, a reporting solution or algorithm and then working hard to try and get the assumed end customer of that to use it. Convincing people to adopt a solution becomes the focus, not solving the customer need. Instead, the management of data as a product starts with the problem that users have and are trying to solve and then prioritises working in collaboration with the end customer on a data product that is needed. The person you are building for is baked into the answer, they want it.'[13]

Treating data as a product requires a new way of thinking, new approaches to delivering data solutions and new roles to manage your outputs. We cover this through the book to help you embed this mentality and approach.

---

13 Interview with Anne-Claire Baschet, 29 November 2020

Data as a service

Service is intangible. Service is taking action to create value for someone else. That action is the experience, expertise and understanding of providing a set of data services. This is the role of the data team. The data team are helping to federate data capability into the organisation through the defined set of services created to solve a business need.

It is important to understand that a product may need some services to be useful or be part of the overall offering. Let's use the example of data quality. The data quality service includes data profiling, a quality assessment, monitoring and reconciliation and finally remediation. We have labelled it a service because there is a need for the data team to provide expert advice, guidance and training and to help create data quality rules for the business. What are the components of the service and do they include any products?

Let's look at the parts to better understand our data services and products for data quality. Data profiling allows the business to understand the data and focus on the attributes that may need attention. Let's say our business outcome is ensuring the address of the customer is correct. You will ideally use a data product to profile the data, a data quality profile dashboard, for example. The activity of setting up the tool and training the business user how to profile their data is an example of the service. If all fields in the address are of good quality except postcode then you focus on defining how to fix postcode. Profiling has allowed you to narrow the scope of the activity needed to meet the business outcome of a valid customer address.

The quality assessment may include reviewing the process, defining critical data, looking to identify owners and determining any data which may need profiling completed. These activities need someone who can run workshops, interpret business jargon and understand how ownership works. This is a pure service offering.

Monitoring will likely be undertaken by providing a dashboard with regular updates and thresholds to ensure whatever business context the data is used for is fit for purpose. This will be an ongoing activity, undertaken by a business user who should be self-sufficient, ie can access their dashboards (product) and identify action needed to ensure their business outcome is met.

By using a set of products and services, we have started to ensure we improve a business outcome; with ownership in place, we have increased account-ability and documented a key process so it can be simplified or at a minimum understood and maintained. The business users utilise data products and services to be independent from the data team. We are effectively federating out data responsibility in the business, which is becoming data-guided.

In the smoothie example, a service could be delivering the raw materials. It could be training and servicing the commercial blender so the shop can make and sell the smoothie. The key point here is that data services and products are often synergistic. This is especially true in the data space where the value is in a combined set of services and products.

Introducing the Level Up Framework

Having worked with hundreds of organisations across the private, public and third sectors, it is clear to us that certain activities are consistently required to create the kind of success that the data 'brand' promises. Time and again we have seen the same blockers and challenges inhibiting organisations from meeting expectations. There is frustration and anxiety from business and data leaders about what to do first, which order to proceed in, how quickly to progress certain elements and how to make success more certain. While every situation is different, there is commonality in the building blocks and activities that are required as you progress to becoming an organisation that is truly data-guided.

The Level Up Framework is a method we have developed to make the journey more practical, more predictable and easier to explain. It removes the fog and brings clarity to what you need to do, in what order and to what end. The framework values business outcomes and building capabilities in equal measure but prioritises an approach that focuses (to the point of obsession) on adding incremental business value. It has taken learning from the start-up philosophy and digital native organisations and applied these through the lens of the data journey.

The Level Up Framework is based on five broad stages that provide activities to carry out and the criteria that tell you when you are ready to go to the next stage. Each stage builds on the last and, the better you achieve the criteria of one stage, the more certain and likely you are of success in the subsequent stage. This book breaks down these stages, giving clarity about what you should be thinking about, what you should be doing and how best to punch through to the next stage.

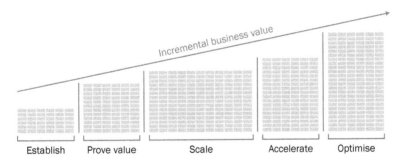

Establish   Prove value   Scale   Accelerate   Optimise

The Level Up Framework

Here are the stages of the framework:

- **Stage 1 – Establish:** set the agenda for data in your organisation, and get buy-in and initial funding. Optimum duration: 3–6 months.

- Educate the organisation
- Identify the business need
- Create a starter team
- Build the case and get initial investment
- Communication and collaboration

- **Stage 2 – Prove Value:** build credibility and prove the value of data by delivering business value/ return, building foundational capabilities and refining the roadmap. Optimum duration: 3–6 months.

  - Build an MVP that delivers small value
  - Create visibility of core business metrics
  - Establish technology practice
  - Get investment to scale
  - Communication and collaboration

- **Stage 3 – Scale:** deliver business value at scale across the organisation and cement your core capabilities. Optimum duration: 6–12 months.

  - Deliver big business returns
  - Scale data products and services
  - Grow skills and organisation design
  - Mature the operating model
  - Embed data-guided culture
  - Communication and collaboration

- **Stage 4 – Accelerate:** shorten the time to market for business outcomes at scale through data products and service. Optimum duration: value-driven.

- Deliver fast business returns
- Build strategic optimum organisation
- Implement event-driven and automated actions
- Incremental, rapid innovation
- Continuous improvement/learning

- **Stage 5 – Optimise:** refine and optimise processes, outcomes and results. Optimum duration: ad infinitum.
  - Focus on optimisation of process and outcomes
  - Think small adjustments, huge returns
  - Hands-free decision-making
  - Valued data asset
  - No decisions made without data

Graeme McDermott, chief data officer at Tempcover (and formerly Addison Lee and the AA), says:

'The data profession tends to attract certain stereotypes or, as we prefer to call them, "segments". One being the introverted, conscientious, highly ordered, detailed, 100% right data analyst. I was, and still am on some days, one of them, and I won't be alone. The problem is when someone gives you some data, it's never up to the standards you would set yourself if the boot was on the other foot. Trust me, I've seen data professionals send data to others; it's like a military exercise of precision and comprehensiveness. Imagine applying this to all your data and it becomes a life's work to rectify or, worse, they give up trying. It took me a while to realise that it will kill you trying to aim for a destination of perfection in one go, to try to boil the ocean. I soon realised that data is not a destination, but a journey with several waypoints on the way. You need to set, and expect to vary, the waypoints that act as smaller achievable destinations along that journey. Remember to look back and reward yourself with how far you've come also.'[14]

---

14 Interview with Graeme McDermott, 23 November 2020

PART 2

GETTING OFF THE GROUND

Like a new boss at a sports club who lays out their vision for the club, the style of play they want to create, the expectations they have of their team, the way they treat the support staff and the communication and passion they build with the fans, the early stages of your journey are critical to your success or failure. Don't underestimate the importance of getting off on the right foot and its impact on your ability to drive business value.

Building strong foundations will provide you with a clear message about your intentions to create stand-out value from data. Get this stage right and you will set yourself up much better than those who jump straight to hiring twenty data scientists, buying the most expensive technology on the market and trying to implement the latest machine learning.

In this section we will be covering the first two stages of the Level Up Framework: Establish the Agenda and Prove Value. As in the early stages of a start-up, you'll be understanding your customers, building your community, defining your proposition, assessing your market fit, securing early investment, building credibility, proving value to your customers and stakeholders and educating your audience on the upsides of this journey.

At the end of each of the first four stages of the Level Up Framework, we also share what we call the 'break-through criteria', which act as a guide on what you should achieve by the end of each stage to punch through to the next stage successfully.

TWO

Establish The Agenda

Let's get something clear. You aren't doing this for the sake of it. You aren't doing it because you read in *The Economist* that 'data is the new oil' (it isn't by the way). You aren't doing it because your neighbour at a barbecue told you how they delivered ten times the return from implementing some artificial intelligence into their marketing funnel. You aren't doing it for fear of missing out (FOMO). These factors may be motivators but they aren't your main reasons.

You are doing this for real, meaningful and transformational impact for you, your business, your shareholders, your stakeholders, your employees and most importantly the customers that your organisation serves.

The mindset needed during this stage is all about understanding the impact data can have and how that aligns itself to your business goals. It's about creating desire and excitement about how much better things can be if you use data effectively in your decision-making. You need to be thinking like a leader. You're campaigning. You're setting out your aspirations. Most importantly, you're listening. You're collaborating and being consultative. You're out building business relationships with the people who own the key metrics of the business and those that can influence those metrics.

Visionary leadership is needed to build excitement, momentum, desire and a thirst for business growth through the use of data and analytics. The board needs to hear how this impacts the future of the company and its outcomes. Department heads need to know how their world will be impacted if they apply data to it.

Think about a brand that you love. Nike. Apple. Brewdog. Your local coffee shop. You're behind them, right? You love what they do, how they do it, what they stand for. You get them. You tell your friends about them. You feel part of the community. This is the mindset needed and the brand you want to create around the agenda you want to put in place.

This stage, establishing the agenda, is exactly that. It's getting clarity about the opportunity for the organisation, developing an understanding of how well set up the business is to achieve that opportunity and creating an agile and iterative plan for what is required.

This chapter is going to give you clarity over the way you establish that agenda, with pace and certainty, to build your solid foundations.

It's a bit of a mess

The funny thing about data is that even if you haven't consciously or strategically tried to sort it out before, it's still likely that huge investment has already been made in it.

Think about your finance department and the hours spent pulling spreadsheets together to report on figures for the board. Think about the marketing team, who have invested in a third party to cobble together some of your customer data and apply it with external data to help build insight. How about the operations team, who hire people to build reports to help understand broken processes? Don't forget the customer services team, who are buying data from an agency to better understand the sentiment of brands like yours. Or the pricing team, who hired a bunch of data scientists to improve the pricing models and a load of technology to help. How about the IT department, who have created a team of developers to build applications and dabble with that endless data warehouse project but for some reason just don't get data?

You are already 'doing data'. Guaranteed. It's just that at this stage it's likely to be a bit of a mess. No coordination. No direction. Huge duplication. Data empires being built all over the place. The wrong skills doing the wrong jobs. Inefficient technology procurement and multiple tools doing the same task. A perception (or reality) that the quality of data is terrible and no data management in place to assure it. No one knows who owns the data. Multiple definitions of sales and 30% of every management meeting spent discussing which sales figure is correct. Does any of this sound familiar? In many organisations this will be a common story.

The biggest problem with all this is the difficulty it creates in trying to make good decisions based on good data and taking action based on those decisions, without which you may as well pack up and go home. This makes the starting point particularly challenging and, unlike a start-up, you have this legacy to deal with and history to untangle.

Educate and tell stories

Most people 'get' that data has an important part to play in business. What's less common is a clear understanding of how it can impact an organisation, in a way that people can really buy into.

At the top level you need to paint a picture about where this can all go. How your industry currently is and could be impacted by data and analytics. Think about the legal sector and the impact automated decisions could have on judges and lawyers. How about farmers and the way they assess crops, their quality, the soil composition? The music, film and entertainment industry, the way people consume content and the role data can play in the creation and serving of that content. It's important that your organisation can make an informed decision on whether you lead the way, follow others or ignore it completely, although we don't recommend the latter option.

You need to show the art of the possible with data. Have you taken your leadership team and key stakeholders to the market-leading players or data and digital native organisations to see how they use data to potent effect? If you're in the public sector and engaging with citizens, have you talked to retailers and brands about how they use data to better understand customer behaviour to drive engagement? How about getting the market-leading technology vendors in front of your organisation to share stories from around the world of how data is being used for commercial, societal and personal benefit?

This all helps to set the scene and build some excitement behind the opportunity, demonstrate what good looks like and deliberately build towards that.

It is equally important to establish specific opportunities within your business, how data can play a part and the impact it can have. You must communicate clearly how data enables your business objectives. Vision is great but unless people can touch and feel what it means to them today, tomorrow and down the line, it can feel out of reach for your business and demotivate rather than inspire. This should form part of an overarching strategy for how you will achieve those business opportunities.

Build out your strategy

Your strategy should act as a framework that describes how you will deliver business value through the application of data and analytics. We discuss our six-pillar approach to defining a data strategy in Part 4; however, we have summarised the main focus areas for the pillars here.

Your strategy should set a north star for your business. A place that you are aiming to get to. A vision that describes in a sentence or two why you are doing what you are doing. It should help to articulate, in plain language, the purpose behind what you will do.

What would this be for your organisation? How about using data to transform the lives of your customers? What about sharing insights with your business partners to build strong, long-lasting relationships? Or what about improving decision-making so that products and services best match the demands of your citizens?

Your strategy should also articulate which parts of your business strategy data will be focused on supporting. This is critical. Your strategy is about identifying the parts of your business data can be used to improve. It's a business strategy and should first and foremost talk about business outcomes. You should be looking to identify business problems or opportunities to focus on, along with the size of the prize. For example, this could be about increasing customer acquisition, removing blockers in business processes or improving pricing for your products or services. It could be putting a price tag on your data for external monetisation. It could be about reducing the cost of running the business or, in regulated businesses, ensuring you're compliant. These use cases are the pots of gold that form the basis of your investment case and are key to establishing your agenda.

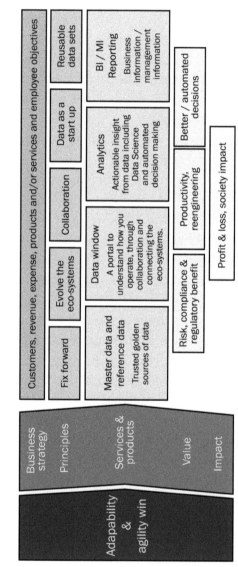

Sample data strategy on a page

Data evangelist Pete Williams says:

> 'Every business is driven by a commercial strategy. Even a "data" business is selling the data it generates. So your data strategy must be an informer and an enabler of the business outcomes. As such it must be closely tied to the success factors of each of the "C" suite responsibilities for them to care. The challenge is getting to speak to them often and in enough detail to help them to understand and want to sponsor your ideas. A tech focused data strategy will exist in a fragile bubble that will burst as soon as times are challenging. A commercially focused data strategy forms an effective shelter to help survive the bad times but take advantage of the good when they come.'[15]

The vision and these use cases are top priority. The rest of your strategy and approach hang off these and ensure you are focused on adding incremental value to the organisation.

To define what changes you need to make that will allow you to deliver those use cases, you will need to understand your existing capabilities and how much value is currently being delivered from data. This means looking at your team, skills, the organisational structure, how you work, the technologies in place and how well they are set up, the way you

---

15 Interview with Pete Williams, 23 November 2020

manage and govern data and how culturally aligned the mindset of your business is to make best use of data. It's good to see how you stack up against others in your industry that you consider your competition so you have a benchmark. Naturally, blockers will pop out during an assessment like this, but be careful not to make too many assumptions about what is and isn't possible.

Technology is a fundamental enabler for success with data, so gain a clear understanding of the organisation's general technology strategy and what decisions have already been made about data and analytics tools. The guidelines, no-go areas and key principles of the technology strategy and main gaps to plug are important to get clear. You'll use this to inform some of the bigger investments required. However, as you will see in the next stage, we don't believe it's right to run into big technology investments until you have proved you can deliver incremental business value.

With the direction set and a clear understanding of the capability gaps that exist, you need to define your roadmap for how you will deliver business value and build the necessary capabilities in the coming months and years. The Level Up Framework gives you a structure for this roadmap.

Your data strategy should be used as a communication tool – a narrative to explain where you are heading and how you will get there. It's not a bible, but a roadmap that steers your journey, gets adjusted as required and against which progress is measured.

Understand stakeholder buy-in

Data shouldn't be in a silo. Business value from data will almost certainly not be limited to one team, one business problem or one area of your organisation. Data (and its value) is pervasive and prevalent in every customer interaction, every system key stroke, every employee connection. As the world becomes more digital, this paradigm is increasingly important.

The opportunity that exists can be applied to most parts of your business. Nearly all the people in your organisation are your stakeholders. This is a unique challenge for data strategies. Possibly the only other area in the business like that is human resources (HR), with which everyone will have need to have some interaction.

Stakeholder engagement and more importantly buy-in are critical to your success overall but particularly at these burgeoning stages of the journey. At a minimum you will need to understand the relative buy-in of the key budget-holders, decision-makers and influencers in the organisation.

Buy-in can be understood from two angles: (1) clarity and understanding of the business outcome and (2) experience and evidence of the outcome that data can give to that individual or the organisation as a whole. The matrix below is a way to plot buy-in of the key stakeholders and then put in appropriate interventions that ensure you have the right commitment from the right people.

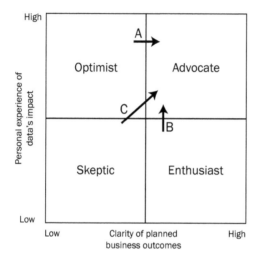

Stakeholder buy-in matrix

This produces four types of people associated with their level of buy-in:

- **The optimist:** they have seen data add value before so they get it and are up for it but don't yet know what value it will add to this company.

- **The enthusiast:** they understand what value data can add to the company and are keen to make it happen but they have no personal experience of it working. We could call them cautious optimists.

- **The skeptic:** they have never seen data work for a business and don't get how it can for your business. These are clearly the least bought in.

- **The advocate:** they have seen it work before, understand how it can add value to your business and have properly bought in to what you are trying to achieve.

A different approach will be needed for each of these groups and you should ensure you have enough advocates to help punch through to the next stage.

Create a starter team

You will need to build your minimum efficient organisation. That is, the leanest possible team to ensure you can effectively get through this stage and be prepared to move at pace through the next stage, Prove Value.

This stage and team are best led by someone with relative seniority within the organisation. Someone who can own the definition and execution of a business-focused strategy. Someone who can engage and influence people across the business and position effectively to the board and senior leadership team. The chief data officer is a role that could take this responsibility and has grown in importance recently as companies try to get a handle on their data strategy. We explore the role of the CDO further in Part 4. Those without a CDO will still need to ensure they have someone in the organisation able to set and lead the strategy. Without this capability it is tough to get any traction.

Whoever takes that data leadership responsibility will want to build a team with the energy, focus and passion to truly understand and care for the business outcomes and a culture of developing high-performing, innovative and agile teams. A crack team that can roll up their sleeves and get things done. You'll want to start small and grow out from this team so they will set the tone for how your data-focused crew operate. Regardless of what level your organisation is at, data needs leadership at a top level to get traction and momentum. Changes need leadership.

Since part of the point of this stage is to define future roles, responsibilities and organisational structure, to some degree where this team sits is not important. What is important is that they are given autonomy and support to help shape the agenda and break down silos.

Build the case and get investment

You need to know how big an impact data can make on your organisation and where that impact could be felt. Is this a £1, £1 million or £100 million opportunity? Have you worked out which elements of the business strategy you can impact and at what scale?

Hidden within your organisation are pots of gold that can help improve your key business metrics. By applying data-guided thinking, there will be opportunities to increase your revenues, reduce the cost of your operations, build stronger relationships with partners and suppliers, understand and engage your employees and customers, build better products and enter new markets.

Knowing the size of the prize is critical. Once we know, we need to be able to articulate this alongside the investment required. Many data initiatives are focused on developing data capabilities within the organisation (like data governance, building technology platforms, recruiting data scientists) and not on delivering incremental value. The size of the prize is often a forgotten piece when asking for investment.

You may even get budget approved this way but this will undoubtedly cause issues further along the journey when money has been invested and no return has been felt.

Your organisation will have its own internal process for approving expenditure, deciding whether that spend is operating expenditure (OPEX) or capital expenditure (CAPEX), budget cycles, investment proposals, return on investment (ROI) or internal rate of return (IRR) hurdles to hit. You should lay some groundwork ahead of those formal discussions by telling the story in a way that effectively conveys your message about your case and investment requirements.

This is a sales pitch. You are trying to get your organisation behind the outcome you are confident you can achieve, sell those benefits and make it clear you have a well thought out plan to move the agenda forward. You should think about this like a start-up goes about getting angel, seed or series funding. You need a pitch deck and you should spend time looking at formulas that work for getting your pitch right. The table below shows headings and descriptions that you should consider including in your budget request presentation.

Vision	This is a one-sentence overview of what you are looking to achieve and the value you expect to bring to the organisation. It's your 'elevator' pitch. Keep it short, simple and jargon-free. This is your why, your purpose for doing this.
Business opportunity	Use this slide to articulate the total size of the opportunity. Be as broad as possible but frame it in terms of the business strategy and try to break it down into areas of the business you can address with data. Be clear on what return is available. This is you focusing on what you can genuinely achieve.

The problem	Use this section to summarise why the organisation struggles to reach this business opportunity. What's stopping you from achieving the prize now? Try to tell a relatable story about the challenges to make the problem as real as possible and how it impacts your goals. Don't get too far into the weeds.
The solution	Now you can start talking about the how. You will be tempted to put this earlier in the presentation but resist that. You get to dive into describing the capabilities you will need to put in place across the business. You are describing how the solution helps remove problems to achieve the business opportunity.
Roadmap	You should use this section to show, ideally on a single page, your plan for achieving the solution and therefore the business opportunities. Be pragmatic and realistic about this and have your assumptions ready so you can explain how the plan is made up.
Investment needs	You're now in a position to explain your investment requirements. You will want to explain how much you think you will need across your planning horizon, how much you need to get through the next stage of the Level Up Framework (Prove Value), how you will be spending the money and how it contributes to the goals.

Industry benchmark (optional)	Stories from your competitors or similar organisations in different industries can be a great way to show whether you are behind, ahead or in line with where your industry is. This kind of comparison isn't for everyone; use it carefully to help the overall story and not distract from your message. You should apply this at the relevant point in the presentation depending on the comparison, for example how your opportunity compares, how your problems compare and so on.

Communication as an agent for change

The ability of any leader to collaborate and build relationships is critical to their success. This is underpinned by their ability to communicate well. Strong, regular and clear communication at this stage is a sure-fire way to get off the ground and set yourself up for success. Using everything you have learned in this chapter on education, defining a strategy, engaging stakeholders, getting your team together and building and sharing your pitch deck all require some epic communication skills.

At this point, and throughout this journey, it's important to remember that people engage with messages in different ways. The format and approach used need to be considered depending on the audience, the message and the communication channel. The twenty-slide PowerPoint presentation used in a meeting may not land well with everyone if sent via email or stored on your intranet.

Think about the lens you put on what you are communicating. The chief finance officer will need a different lens on the strategy to the chief technology officer. They will need a different lens to an analytics team or the line of department leads. One size doesn't fit all and tailoring the approach, personalising the message and targeting your communication will help to ensure you establish a strong agenda.

Giving people options for how they consume content helps maximise engagement and increases the chances of your message landing and being understood. Get creative. Use videos, blogs, demonstrations, newsletters, articles, animations, show and tells, Q&A and 'ask me anything' sessions. This is about communicating your message, building credibility, building a culture of sharing and collaboration, getting buy-in and ensuring your strategy is clear and understood.

Establish the Agenda: the breakthrough criteria

There are a number of must-have outcomes you need to have reached by the end of this stage. These outcomes give you what you need in order to punch through to the next stage and ensure strong foundations are in place.

1. **Organisational buy-in:** at this stage you are looking for enough buy-in from the organisation to ensure you have people who are interested and rooting for success. We're talking emotional buy-in – some top down, some bottom up.

2. **Strategic backing:** success with data needs to be of strategic importance, aligned to the business goals and of significance to the success of the organisation.

3. **Pots of gold identified:** you need to know where the best opportunities or challenges are, what the size of the prize is and what the relative priorities are.

4. **Minimum efficient organisation in place:** the right team ready to deliver the Prove Value stage.

5. **Pitch deck:** bringing together the vision, strategy, pots of gold and investments required into a solid story, tailored to the audience with the right lens.

6. **Investment required:** you will have assessed the costs necessary to deliver the strategy and a roadmap of investments you are likely to make along the way.

7. **Plan for the Prove Value stage:** a clear plan for the next stage of the journey. What will you do next?

8. **Funding for the Prove Value stage:** you'll want enough funding to prove value, refine your plan and start building capability.

THREE

Prove Value

In October 2007, Brian Chesky and his roommate Joe Gebbia were unemployed and looking for a way to make some extra cash to pay rent. There was a major shortage of hotel rooms and traditional accommodation in San Francisco as there were several conferences coming up.

Chesky and Gebbia decided to rent out part of their apartment to people struggling to find somewhere to stay. They put together a basic website called airbedandbreakfast.com, which offered an airbed in their loft and a homemade breakfast the following morning for $80 per night.

Over the next eleven years and after some early failed attempts to scale the business, get the proposition right and secure investment, Airbnb scaled to a $31 billion valuation and secured $4.4 billion investment. It is a global phenomenon.

Three people showed up in October 2007, which proved to the founders that they had a proposition. No big investment. No extensive business case. No investment in a huge team to start the idea. No major technology platform. Just a concept that needed testing and proof that they could get value from something.

According to Chesky, 'people have said that [Airbnb is] the worst idea that ever worked.'[16] They proved that there was a demand for what seemed at the time like a crazy idea. On the face of it, letting a stranger into your house to stay overnight sounded like a ridiculous idea. Who would want to offer that? Who would want to stay?

Airbnb and many other start-ups like it have shown us that it's worth proving value before starting to scale, get or make big investments. Until the founders landed on the right business model that worked, proved successful and showed that the idea was credible, they couldn't take it forward, big or fast. Getting data right needs this same mentality and approach.

---

16 C Garing, 'Airbnb founder: Company "wasn't supposed to be the big idea"', *Vanity Fair*, 10 October 2014, www.vanityfair.com/news/tech/2014/10/airbnb-founder-big-idea-logo

Gaining credibility

The hard work during Establish the Agenda was all about getting clarity on the potential opportunity for your organisation, understanding how well set up the business is to achieve that opportunity and creating an agile and iterative plan.

Armed with your initial funding, this next step is to do what Chesky and Gebbia did and prove value. Before pushing hard on further deep investments, it's vital that you gain credibility by demonstrating that applying data to known and necessary business challenges can add value to the business.

If your aim is to create a business guided by data, the journey you go on should apply that concept. Use evidence that proves as an organisation you can make this work before you decide to press on. While you want to aim for the best possible return, it's likely that you'll make small gains and small returns compared to what was previously defined as the size of the prize. This is fine and expected. It's what you want, really – small investment, prove you can get a return and create some data points of success.

During this stage you'll be looking to further validate your assumptions on your strategy and pivot accordingly. As you learn and start this process there will be blockers, changes and recruitment challenges so we need to keep an eye on the next move and not be afraid to change our approach.

What's important is the business outcome. The route will change and your plans will change. Openness and honesty, coupled with positive delivery, help to build credibility and trust that you know what you are doing and why. Working alongside and in collaboration with your peers and colleagues at this stage will not only help gain credibility but also build relationships and pave the way for easier and sharper communication when things change or don't go to plan.

New concepts need a new mindset

The concept of proving value, starting small and then scaling is alien to many, particularly when it comes to securing budget, so this stage should aim to embed this mindset into the organisation. There will be many new ways of working for technology teams, for data teams, for how commercial teams engage and this is the stage where you can start to embed a new cultural mindset.

This is the mindset we want you to have during this whole journey, not just at this stage. Start small, prove value, then scale, accelerate and optimise. Prove first then take an idea forward, whether you are building a dashboard, launching a data product, taking a new proposition to market, or building a data flow or new algorithm. It's the best way to prove that something is heading in the right direction and worth investing in before jumping in and increasing spend.

Ultimately you build the right thing faster, rather than taking a long time to build something big that was never going to work in the first place.

Build and activate a data product

The problem with the way organisations have traditionally tried to get off the ground with data strategies is that they focus on building perfect solutions from the start with no clear set of business use cases. They get investment to build a company-wide data warehouse and start bringing data together, building data models and dashboards based on user requirements. The challenge here is that there is no link to the changes the business will make or the outcomes they're looking to achieve. It's more like a technology platform with no purpose, rather than a business solution with real impact.

Packaging up a business outcome, the technology and the data required to support that outcome means we need to start thinking about the planning and execution of solutions through a product development lens and moving from data solutions to data products. This product-centric approach allows you to scale individual and isolated successes into sustainable, organisation-wide, data-guided decisions that need to be the foundation of your data strategy.

We discuss the product development approach and roles required elsewhere in this book but for now the important part is that this stage of the journey requires you to prove value and credibility by identifying a challenge or problem, developing a solution and taking steps to achieve some of the business value associated with it. A mechanism that allows for rapid iteration and adjustments that mean you can change the solution as you learn how it impacts the business.

You should pick one of the use cases identified at the Establish stage (for example: improve customer retention, increase open rates on emails, reduce the time to carry out a process) and one that can be developed at low cost to quickly determine whether you can achieve the improvements you believed were possible. This is about proving to yourself, your business and your stakeholders that by applying data to a decision and therefore a business outcome, you can make some improvements, or at the very least learn that you can't.

When you pick a use case, it's important to think about the end outcome you are trying to impact. The data product doesn't stop at the development of a solution but at the implementation of a change that impacts the end customer, stakeholder or process. Consider a few use cases to decide which you think is the most feasible because of access to the data, the technology and the skills required, balanced against the value that is potentially achievable.

Once you have this use case identified, you should be looking to build a starter data product to achieve it. Not one with all the bells and whistles but an MVP or solution that brings together the data, builds a basic data model and delivers insight that can be acted upon. Being acted upon is the vital component to validate that you have been able to move a needle and get some of the business value associated with the use case.

Think of what you are building here as a prototype or a test. A test for new ways of working. A test that you can treat data as a product. A test of bringing people together and collaborating in ways they may have not before. A test of achieving improvements to your chosen use case. These factors come together to try to achieve a result and in the process prove value and gain credibility.

The aims of this initial data product build are that you impact your business outcomes in some way, learn from it and can demonstrate and communicate all this to the business stakeholders. You will use this MVP and others like it as a basis for growth in the next stages of the framework.

This idea of building an MVP or starter data product is summarised nicely by Jagpal Jheeta, a business and technology director with experience across organisations such as Marks & Spencer, Symphony EYC, Royal Mail and the Financial Conduct Authority:

> 'In business, as in life, we make progress by connecting and collaborating, bringing together the best ideas from our networks, testing, scaling and industrialising as fast as possible. Data enables us to do this. We need to be selective and focus on a few initiatives that can move the dial, while understanding those that don't, and stopping those. Identifying the winners and accelerating those initiatives can only happen with the right data, at the right time, in the hands of those that can make decisions.'[17]

Rapid provision of insights

During these early stages of your journey, you are likely to come up against resistance to anything new around analytics, algorithms, the potential of AI and exciting use cases if your stakeholders are unable to get reports that tell them how the company performed last week. For all the exciting benefits that you know are waiting to be unlocked, there is no getting away from the fact that everyone will want access to reports

---

17 Interview with Jagpal Jheeta, 20 November 2020

and dashboards that give them better clarity over the key metrics of the organisation.

Visibility of metrics is vital to an organisation's ability to understand where it has come from, know how it is performing today and see indications of what may be coming down the line. This is the lifeblood of a leadership team's ability to understand whether the actions and strategies they have in place are impacting the outcomes. There will always be a thirst for these macro-level insights. At this stage of the journey, when you should be looking to prove value and build credibility, it is sensible to allocate some focus to rapidly providing data products that support this thirst.

There are several issues to watch out for:

1. Reports add limited value if they aren't aligned to key outcomes.

2. People often don't know what they need until they see it so it's possible that you could spend hours building reports and dashboards that never get used.

3. Unless you have actively ensured that metric definitions are agreed, you can end up creating more problems than you solve.

4. It can be hard to prioritise where to invest time and which metrics to build.

5. It can be challenging to deliver clean, accurate metrics as the underlying data work required has yet to be carried out.

All of these 'watch outs' can lead to big investments in 'sorting out core reporting' with limited value or overall benefit to the agenda.

What's needed is the rapid provision of insights that prioritise the most impactful metrics and deliver those as data products to the stakeholders who have the biggest influence over the performance of that metric. Even though the objective is to deliver insights, you are still looking to focus on the things that could have the biggest impact on the outcomes of the business. Focus on the outcomes and actions you want to drive rather than the report/dashboard itself. The destination is the change and not the data product (dashboard) itself.

The other valuable step that can be taken is to unlock data access to the analysts or data scientists in the organisation so they can gain insights themselves. There is often a concern about this as it may mean you are creating duplication of effort or new cottage industries. But with good governance this can be a valuable way to accelerate getting data in the hands of the right people and not creating new blockers.

Putting in place foundational capabilities

While the priority for this stage is to prove value by getting hands dirty and building data products focused on business outcomes, it's also the time to start building the capabilities that will form the basis of your data strategy. Capabilities should be built relative to where you are in the journey and the level of incremental business value that you have delivered at that stage.

You aren't yet ready to swamp the organisation with new technology, teams of data scientists, data engineers or other roles as you are still in the process of proving value. What's needed is a next iteration of growing out your capabilities – a first fix. Remember we talked about getting seed funding as part of the Establish stage? Along with the investment in some early data products, these capabilities are what you want to invest in further during this stage.

The key foundational capabilities to consider at this stage of your journey cover:

1. Building your minimum efficient organisation

2. Initiating your new approach and ceremonies

3. Putting in place starter technology and architecture that can scale

4. Communication: the rule of seven

Building your minimum efficient organisation

You need to enhance your team so that you can deliver this stage but also be ready to move into the Scale phase of the Level Up Framework. This will build on the starter team put in place during Establish, and the mix implemented there will change what you look to bring together here. You want to be building your 'minimum efficient organisation' at this stage – the smallest team required to build and activate the data product and rapid insights mentioned earlier.

Consider the following groups of skills that will form the basis of what's needed to build those data products and further prepare the organisation. Note that these are groups of discipline rather than names of roles.

Business discovery

Having a team that's able to engage with the broader business to understand how it operates – the processes, the key metrics, what's important to the leaders and front-line staff – is critical to delivering outcomes and data products that have impact. The disciplines required are as follows:

- **Product management** is the practice of strategically driving the development, launch and continual support and improvement of your organisation's data products.

- **Business analysis** enables change by understanding problems and opportunities, defining needs and recommending solutions that deliver value. They are agents of change.

- **Business enablement** works to ensure that the organisation is ready, educated and able to understand data in a way that helps them make decisions, implement change and create action.

Delivery

Visions or strategies without a plan are just ideas and aspirations, and a plan without action is just a nice Gantt chart, product backlog or Kanban board. The delivery discipline comprises the skills required to get the development of data products and technology solutions planned, designed, built and delivered.

- **Architecture and design** make up the practice of strategically defining the technology, tools, underlying architecture and design required to deliver the organisation's data products.

- **Engineering** is the craft that develops and tests the solution underpinning the data products, including building data pipelines and structured data sets.

- **Data science** allows rules, mathematical models and scientific methods to be applied to data to identify patterns and insights, and builds models to feed your data products.

- **Analytics and business intelligence** help to answer business questions by visualising data and solving business problems.

Data management

Data management is foundational to the success of not only data strategy but also an organisation's ability to interact effectively with its people, products, customers, operations and money. This discipline helps to ensure the delivery of trustworthy data for the business, ready to be harnessed to generate value. We do this by driving an ownership model that aligns to the risk framework of the organisation and supports the connection, capture and understanding of the organisation's ecosystem.

- **Assurance** is the practice of defining and implementing steps to assure data in terms of its quality, consistency, accuracy, timeliness and accessibility through the end-to-end data value chain.

- **Protection** is the practice of putting in place controls to protect an organisation's data assets in terms of physical and cyber security controls.

- **Adherence** is the work required to ensure the process of assurance and protection is adhered to.

You may be bringing people in from outside your organisation, either through recruitment, contracting or consultancy. You may be consolidating from across your organisation or you may be cross-training people to carry out these functions. The decision here will depend on the preferred approach, pace of change you'd like to move at or what you are used to.

One example of this type of this organisation was developed by Ryan den Rooijen, the Chief Data Officer of Chalhoub Group, the leading luxury retailer in the Middle East. Ryan stated:

> 'When I started in my role I was keen to hit the ground running. Therefore, instead of building a lot of siloed teams centered around capabilities, eg data engineering, data science, etc. I instead established three pillars focused on outcomes: Assets, Products and Impact.
>
> **Data Assets** are tasked with ensuring data quality, architecture and management.
>
> **Data Products** identifies opportunities for products and then delivers them end to end.
>
> **Analytics Impact** focuses on delivering operational transformation and profitability.

This model's emphasis on outputs enabled us to quickly deliver business value, while simplifying stakeholder communications. Everyone could understand what the team did.

Additionally, by recruiting "bottom up" we were able to demonstrate progress every step of the way as we grew the team, instead of waiting for our leadership to be recruited before starting."[18]

Initiating your new approach and ceremonies

The way you operate and your approach to planning and tracking progress establish early on that you will be focused on: i) action, ii) scaling out the people involved, and iii) the commitments being made.

To be adaptable and agile, a step change is often required in the approach used to deliver your data strategy. At this early stage it is important to establish this change and set clear team values, culture and behaviours that allow you to work at pace, engage well with the wider business organisation and focus on business outcomes, not just data and technology.

From an objective planning perspective, this means taking the strategy and breaking that down into an overarching one-year goal (for example, deliver

---

18 Interview with Ryan den Rooijen, 2 December 2020

£1 million of business benefit, gain ISO accreditation, sell our data to three of our external stakeholders), then into quarterly outcomes and key results (OKRs), monthly team plans and fortnightly sprints. Maintaining a backlog that is open and shared across the team means you remain focused on the outcomes that align back to the one-year goal and ultimately the business strategy.

We have defined the key concepts and definitions to be used as part of this approach, which prioritises outcomes, communication, collaboration and getting work done over micromanagement, big up-front planning and working in silos. These are as follows:

- **Backlog:** the list of everything that is needed or has been requested that could add value.

- **Backlog refinement:** the practice of improving user stories, acceptance criteria, test cases and other information that is relevant to each backlog item, providing sufficient detail and confidence for the business stakeholder to make informed decisions on the priorities for the next sprint.

- **Business stakeholder:** the person delegated from a business team to work closely with the data team as part of the development process, and responsible for prioritisation. This should be a member of the business unit's leadership team who has a strong commercial understanding and can be trusted to fairly represent interests across the business unit.

- **Daily stand-up:** the daily meeting with everyone associated with the sprint goals. Occurring at the same time each day, it runs for fifteen minutes and takes place regardless of absences. People report what they completed the previous day, what they are working on today and any blockers. New issues are captured. Colleagues can call out areas where help or collaboration are required. This is intended as a quick summary for the team only; it is not a meeting to define solutions or a stakeholder actions meeting.

- **Epic:** a lengthy user story that cannot be completed in one sprint.

- **Show and tell:** a meeting facilitated by the product owner that is used to demonstrate the work completed during the sprint. Business stakeholders and/or end users may attend. Those in attendance agree what has been completed (and what hasn't) so that this can be released to the business.

- **Sprint:** the two-week-long development process during which the team completes tasks to deliver stories and epics.

- **Sprint planning:** a meeting attended by the product owner and the business team. Outside stakeholders may attend as needed. The product owner describes the highest priority features to the team.

- **Sprint retrospective:** a meeting facilitated by the product owner to discuss the sprint and determine what could be changed to make the next sprint more productive.

- **Steering group:** a group of stakeholders who decide on the priority and order of process for the project or workflow programmes that the organisation is delivering. This should consist of some or all of the leadership team for the business unit and could take place as a standing agenda item at a monthly leadership team meeting.

- **Task:** the discrete pieces of work that are required to deliver a story.

- **Theme:** a group of user stories that share a common business goal or objective. For example, if the business objective was to improve customer satisfaction, all the reporting created to support that initiative would be grouped under that theme.

- **User story:** short requirements written from the perspective of an end user. They take the form of: 'As an X, I would like to have Y so that I can do Z.'

- **Workstream alignment:** a monthly meeting of all the data product owners. It is an opportunity for each product owner to provide an update from their area, discuss future work and dependencies and get aligned across the group.

You should also look to establish key performance indicators (KPIs) for the team and data strategy to benchmark and track progress. This keeps you honest and ensures that everyone is aware of the impact they individually have on the outcomes and how collectively you are impacting on the organisation. We cover this in more detail in Part 4.

Putting in place starter technology and architecture that can scale

There can be a temptation to prioritise buying or sorting technology ahead of anything else but there are several things to get right and to put in place before this stage. You may have some data technology already or an existing/legacy technology estate in place. This is either a great thing as you have the technology you need or it is holding you back, depending on the previous choices made. You may be starting from scratch and have little or nothing in place, in which case the technology market will be a daunting place to go fishing in.

Either way, we need to ensure that what we put in place is exactly what is required to move you through the Prove Value stage but has the ability to grow with you into the Scale stage and beyond. You don't need a gold-plated solution that is able to satisfy every requirement you can think of for capabilities needed at the Accelerate or Optimise stages of the Level Up

Framework. If you do that you will be investing in technology that you won't be able to maximise, leading to wasted investment.

You need a starter technology platform that is small, lightweight, low cost and adaptable, with only the components necessary to build and activate your initial data product and to build the rapid insights identified as priority. The aim here is to prove that you can move the needle – not take over the world. Cloud technology has been a key enabler to this approach and should form a key part of your thinking if you want agility and flexibility. Cloud provides the ability to scale up and down as demand changes and enables a smaller investment to get started that can grow and scale as you grow and scale.

The importance of use cases

In designing and building your adaptable data platform, use cases matter. They matter for many reasons but there are three which are key: (1) picking the right technology, (2) helping with prioritisation, and (3) helping make design decisions.

Firstly, without understanding your use cases you can't pick the right technology. If, for example, you don't understand that your marketing team wants to make real-time product recommendations to customers browsing your website, based on their page views, previous purchases and visit history, there is no way you can establish the kind of data platform and infrastructure to support that requirement. That's different from just looking to build some solid business intelligence and reporting capability, for which the architecture and design decisions would be very different.

Secondly, the prioritisation of your use cases makes a huge difference to the order in which you should buy technology and build the architecture. In what order are you going to tackle building your platform? That needs to be aligned to the use cases that are important and the order in which you will deliver them. You will have a vision for what your data platform can achieve but it's unlikely you will need everything on day one. Tie your early decisions about technology and what you implement back to your use cases, identify the most value-driving themes and do those first. This also helps you to unpick the technology market and know which tools you should and shouldn't consider. It can be easy to fall for the sales pitch of the data vendors without properly understanding what you are looking for, why and when. Having that clarity of use case and therefore the functionality you need will help to better articulate need, shortlist technology candidates and make a sensible selection.

Thirdly, all your architectural design decisions are going to come back to the use cases. Choosing technology that can scale, the performance you require from it, the security that you may need in place, the functionality it needs to deliver, the data you need to ingest, the data model you need to build. For all of those decisions you're going to need to refer back to the use cases you're trying to deliver. Without doing this you can end up investing in building a shiny data platform with all the latest functionality and trendiest tech that doesn't meet the needs of the business or, alternatively, a substandard platform that can't deal with the scale, growth or pace of change needed to get the most value from data.

Initiate your starter technology platform

The idea with technology at this stage is to get a starter platform off the ground and set the foundation. This may or may not be technology you already have but the principle of selecting a lightweight, low additional cost platform that can be used to prove value and that can scale is paramount.

During this stage, and to enable you to build your initial data products and rapid insights, you will need to be able to ingest some data sets, for example sales and customer data, store and transform (or model) that data, ensure a level of governance, provide an ability to build dashboards and analyse data and outputs so you can make business decisions. Outcome over perfection is what you are after here and a platform that allows you to do those things will mean you can prove and demonstrate value without investing millions (in implementing new solutions or fixing what you already have) ahead of time.

This won't be your final set-up or platform – you will need to add functionality, add complexity, tighten the governance, allow different workloads to take place – but this is to set you up for success and give you the ammunition required to get investment to start to put more scale and pace through the data products, services and solutions you will want to build next.

The diagram below shows the key functionality required; the level of complexity it can handle will change but this is what is required from day one.

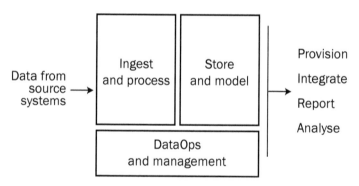

High-level technology capabilities

Your platform should consist of the following high-level capabilities:

- **Ingest and process:** the ability to access, extract and bring together data from various source applications (finance, ERP, CRM, HR, website, supply chain systems, emails, videos, audio files etc) either in regular batch loads of data, near real time in small batches or in real time.

- **Storage:** once you have ingested that data, it will need to be stored in a way that allows it to be accessed when and where required for both operational and innovation reasons.

- **Modelling:** the data you are storing in its raw form will need to be modelled. It will be consolidated, aggregated and improved on by applying models and processing that derive insights, answers to questions and creation of new data and predictions.

- **Access and provision:** the insights and modelled data that are produced will need to be accessed by people and/or other systems, so technology that allows the data to be analysed, reported on and shared with others is required.

- **DataOps and management:** wrapping around all this is the technology needed to better operate, manage, secure and govern the data itself, the process of data movement and the people and systems accessing it.

These high-level capabilities align closely with the data value chain earlier. Your data platform is there to move data through the data value chain so that you can reach value realisation.

Communication: the 'rule of seven'

Repetition is an extremely effective communication strategy. In marketing and advertising it's been proven that consistent messaging over a sustained period to a specific (or target) audience is necessary to build understanding, trust and acceptance of the message and the brand. The 'rule of seven' suggests that consumers need to hear or see a message seven times before they are likely to take action.[19] That's a lot of communication to land a message. While the Establish the Agenda stage focuses on building the strategy, getting buy-in, getting stakeholders on board and ultimately agreement from the organisation to invest and move forward, remember that the communication about what you are trying to achieve, what outcomes you expect and what engagement you need from everyone is still not done. During the Prove Value stage you need to keep communication high, work to maintain engagement with your stakeholders and continue to educate the organisation.

The strategy and roadmap for data should be handled like marketing. Don't leave your strategy papers, slides, videos and infographics gathering dust. Get out to the wider organisation and continue the discussions, remind people of the plan, get champions on board with the journey, share progress updates,

---

19 B Onibalusi, 'Rule of 7: Skyrocket your business growth with this marketing principle', Effective Business Ideas, no date, www.effectivebusinessideas.com/the-rule-of-7

communicate the successes and what you've learned. Consider starting an internal newsletter. Add relevant news from your industry on how data and digital are being maximised, share stories about what's happening within the company, raise the profile of the team driving the agenda. How about running show and tell sessions in other people's team meetings or grabbing a slot at the next board meeting? What about lunch and learn sessions to demonstrate early wins, data products in development or new insights that have been found? The power of easily shareable anecdotes at this stage is strong – use them brazenly.

This all helps to educate, increase understanding and get people behind what you're looking to achieve and the journey you are on. Telling people the strategy once then ploughing on will lose your stakeholders, restrict your ability to prove value and slow you down as you try to move to the Scale stage.

Iterate the roadmap

During Establish the Agenda you will have created a strategy for delivering value from data, identified the capabilities needed and assessed what the roadmap for implementing should be, based on the Level Up Framework. That will have given you enough to get the buy-in and investment required to move to this stage, Prove Value. It may not have answered all the questions and things may have changed – new CEO, global pandemic strikes, someone in your team leaves. You will be learning more about your ability to engender change, conflicts or tension between teams, misalignment of priorities, further challenges on stakeholder engagement and so on.

During this Prove Value stage, alongside building a valuable use case, insights, team and platform you will also need to refine the strategy and roadmap. This will include prioritising the use cases and processes you will be focusing on as part of the next stage of your roadmap. This will allow you to focus on the right problems to solve, processes to fix or business opportunities to go after. Put these use cases into a backlog that can be easily communicated and managed and on a timeline so you have a rough order in which you are likely to tackle them. This shouldn't act as a fixed plan but more as a direction of travel that gets reviewed on a regular basis to ensure the next use case to be worked on is indeed still priority and the right place to invest time, energy and money.

The capabilities required to deliver these use cases for the Scale stage also need refinement to ensure you have solid plans in place for your team, skills, culture, data governance and management, ways of working and technology. Your views may have adjusted through the delivery of your data product and rapid insights and your strategy and plans should reflect that. You are gearing up so that once you have successfully punched through from Prove Value to Scale, you know what to do next.

Most importantly, you need to further refine the investment required to get into and through the Scale stage, in which you push ahead with the delivery of business value and incrementally scale up your capabilities. This starts to require some bigger investments in people, technology and business change. Getting clarity on what's needed in terms of those investments and the expected value that will be returned helps to get enough funding to scale up your operation in a way that your stakeholders understand and are bought into. Build on the pitch deck that was used during the Establish the Agenda stage to get your initial funding. Show what you've been able to achieve, where you are on the journey, lessons you've learned, value you've added and most importantly where you are heading and the use cases you plan to focus on. This needs to be practical and tangible at this stage rather than visionary; you've moved beyond that. That's what will get your investment approved.

Update your pitch deck

During the Establish stage we talked about creating your pitch deck to lay out the story. You are now in a great position to go back with an updated pitch deck summarising progress but also including the validation points you have to back up the assumptions you'd made earlier. You'll also be using this to secure your next round of investment (this would likely be Series A in the world of start-ups) to see you through some or all of the Scale stage of the Level

Up Framework. The table below shows the updated headings and descriptions that you should consider including in this latest budget request presentation.

Vision	A reminder of what you are looking to achieve and the value you expect to bring to the organisation. This is your why, your purpose for doing this, so is unlikely to have changed much.
Business opportunity	Update on the size of the prize you now expect to be able to deliver. You will have some better data to base this on now so can be more confident in your expectations and aspirations.
Early traction	This is an opportunity to summarise the value and learnings you've achieved during this stage. You can use your proof of value and tests you have carried out to show you have been able to deliver on the outcomes articulated last time. You can build some senior credibility through which you'll achieve the buy-in you need.
The problem	Provide an update on what challenges exist in the organisation that prevent you from being able to repeat, reuse, scale and ultimately continue to deliver the valuable outcomes that you've started proving. How far can you get with your existing team and what problems remain?

The solution	Cover how you will deliver more value and which capabilities you need to address to meet the business opportunity. What additional changes do you need to make to continue the positive journey?
Roadmap	Based on learnings to date, update the roadmap to show your plan for the next stage and beyond so it's clear what the journey looks like and what people can expect to see and when.
Investment needs	Now you are asking for investment to get through part or all of the next stage. Be clear on what this ask is, how far it gets you and what your expectations are of the returns.
Technology and platforms (optional)	Since a fair proportion of spend in data strategies is on technology and building platforms, it may be relevant (or required) to explain what choices have been made, what the end state looks like and how far along that journey you are. Some organisations will want to understand your position on cloud, for example, if this is a new concept.
The team (optional)	If you have already invested in new people or moved them around internally to create your initial team, it's often a great idea to introduce the team members and their backgrounds to build credibility that you have the right team (including your own background if this is you putting the case forward!).

Prove Value: the breakthrough criteria

There are some must-have outcomes you need to have reached to punch through to the Scale stage and ensure strong foundations are in place.

1. **Value delivered:** the most important criterion at this stage is that you have proven value to your organisation through delivery of a data product against a use case (or set of use cases) and the delivery of key metrics.

2. **Refined strategy and priorities agreed:** you've built on the strategy and roadmap defined earlier in the journey and refined your focus and priorities.

3. **Organisational buy-in:** you have been able to develop the engagement with the stakeholders, build key allies and generate advocates for what you are trying to achieve.

4. **Minimum efficient organisation in place:** you have a foundational team in place who have helped you get through this stage and who can lead the implementation of the strategy through the Scale stage.

5. **Baseline technology platform implemented:** much of the value from data is enabled by a solid and scalable technology platform and architecture. Your baseline platform will need to be in place. You will also need clarity on how it scales to

support increased data, usage and complexity of requirement.

6. **Investment needed for the Scale stage:** you need to have secured budget to accelerate the development of the capabilities required to deliver against the use cases that support your business strategy.

7. **Your plan for the Scale stage:** you need a clear plan that explains what you will do in the early, mid and latter phases of the Scale stage.

PART 3

GROWTH AND IMPACT

When a start-up moves out of the early stages, they move into scale-up mode. They've developed and tested their proposition, they've got some decent investment behind them, they've built their MVP, had user feedback and started to build their community. They have traction but they aren't yet an established player in their industry. The scale-up mode is critical and focuses on continual innovation, improvements and accelerating growth.

In this part of the book we will be covering the remaining stages of the Level Up Framework – Scale, Accelerate and Optimise. This is your route to establishing data as a critical asset to your business, where you gradually build out the penetration of data into decision-making and improving business outcomes. You've laid strong foundations in the first two stages and earned the right to continue that iterative development towards a capability that works with pace at scale across your organisation.

It's important to maintain the adaptable, agile and iterative approach through these stages. It's far easier to do that in the early stages when the scope is tight and the team and the investments are small.

But the whole ethos of this approach requires you to ensure that you build your strategy around continual improvement, automation where possible and collaborative approaches to data product development.

As before, at the end of each stage of the Level Up Framework we also share what we call the breakthrough criteria, which act as a guide on what you want to achieve to punch through to the next stage successfully.

It's time to up the ante, get data on rails and push on.

FOUR

Scale

We told the story earlier of Chesky and Gebbia, who tested their idea of offering out space in their apartment and proved it was a viable and valuable proposition. To get investment and scale the business, they needed to prove the idea would work. They needed to test several assumptions, like whether strangers would pay to stay in their home, and if strangers would let other strangers stay in their homes too. They had to use early prototypes to test those assumptions and use data and customer feedback to adjust and pivot their idea, the app and the proposition.

Once they had proven that the proposition would work and had a clear idea of what scaling would look like, they were able to secure investment, initially by joining Y Combinator's 2009 winter class and soon after that they received another $600,000 in a seed round from Sequoia Capital and Y Ventures.[20,21] Then they were ready to put their foot to the floor and scale the business. The investment would help them to grow their team, build and test new features and integrations, grow the user base of their app and ultimately disrupt the market.

The Level Up Framework is designed to work in the same way. We urge you not to jump to this stage before you are ready because it's time to put your foot to the floor and scale your data strategy. You are building on the groundwork you put in place during the Establish and Prove Value stages and punching through the wall by hitting the breakthrough criteria. Unless you've done that successfully, there is real danger that you invest big but have missed crucial building blocks like buy-in, stakeholder engagement, a clear strategy and a credible path to success.

This is the meatiest stage of the framework. You are scaling up your team, your technology, the user base, the valuation and impact of your data strategy, the features and functions your data products provide and in the way that you operate. This takes time, energy, focus and commitment but sets you up for the

---

20 M Brown, 'Airbnb: The growth story you didn't know', Growthhackers, no date, https://growthhackers.com/growth-studies/airbnb

21 I Rabang, 'The Airbnb story', Bold Business, 31 May 2019, www.boldbusiness.com/society/airbnb-startup-story

next stage, Accelerate. Enjoy and keep that start-up spirit alive.

To self-service or not to self-service

To become an organisation that is guided by data and one where strategists, leaders and operators have the insight they need to make better decisions, it's easy to see why self-service becomes a panacea for many. The notion that a customer service team, the finance function and your head of HR can pick up their phone, open an app and get answers to their business questions doesn't feel like an unreasonable ask. After years of being dependent on another team (often the IT department), poor tools, slow response to requests and lack of true flexibility, business teams, as one board member put it to us, 'just want the data and we'll do it ourselves'. The win is huge here. Data, and more importantly insights, in the hands of people who can directly change the course of the business, the impact of a project and those making strategic and operational decisions is a sure-fire way of levelling up the returns you get.

Yet this simple-sounding and transformational aspiration is more challenging than it appears, so the question is often raised of whether to implement a self-service approach or not. Let's use an analogy. Prior to online banking, all the work was done for you. You asked someone to carry out an activity and they did the work to make it happen; even simple activities like checking your balance and transferring money required someone else to do that for you.

In 1981, four banks in New York City – Citibank, Chase Manhattan, Chemical Bank and Manufacturers Hanover – tested an innovative way of doing your personal banking through remote services, which made 'home banking' access available for the first time. In 1983, The Bank of Scotland provided its customers with the first ever UK internet banking service, called Homelink, which allowed people to connect to the internet to pay bills and transfer money. Self-service banking was born. By 2006, 80% of US banks offered banking over the internet[22] and by 2020 more than three-quarters of British people used online banking.[23] Even going into a physical branch, we rarely interact with someone else to carry out everyday banking needs. The self-service shift has happened.

Think about the work that must have gone into this shift. The technology changes, the maturity of processes, the automation of data processing, the integration between banks, the global internet infra-structure upgrades, the regulation changes, and so on. Bigger still, how about the cultural shift needed to move people away from visiting branches to doing

22 R Sarreal, 'History of online banking: How internet banking went mainstream', 21 May 2019, GO Banking Rates, www.gobankingrates. com/banking/banks/history-online-banking
23 C Barton, 'Digital banking statistics 2020', Finder, 29 September 2020, www.finder.com/uk/digital-banking-statistics

everything themselves online and through an app? This has required a huge level of education, messaging and marketing to ensure everyone understands how this new self-service approach works. Customer service and technical support teams are on hand to help when things go wrong yet even today many less digitally savvy banking customers struggle to make the shift away from their local branch to carry out transactions. That's a lot of change over thirty years to make this happen.

We aren't saying you need thirty years to move to self-service but we are saying that simply buying a self-service analytics tool or just giving people the data is not going to produce the results you expect overnight without a clear strategy, approach and plan for all the other things talked about in this book.

This doesn't mean it's impossible and that you shouldn't attempt it. Quite the opposite. However, it's a little more nuanced than full self-service or no self-service at all. It's good to think about this in the context of the three main modes business teams can engage with data and insights.

1. **Do it yourself:** business teams can build and carry out the necessary analysis themselves. In this mode the team has all the tools they need, access to the source data, clear guidance on best practice and rules of engagement. They have an understanding of how to apply data to business

decisions and technical skills to make that happen. This is the highest level of self-service.

2. **Do it together:** business teams collaborate with data and insight experts to build and carry out the analysis together. In this mode the team may have some of what's needed in their own team, but not everything. Working on the elements they can and collaborating with others where necessary is effective. For example, dashboards are built by the business team but data modelling is carried out by someone else. This is a hybrid self-service model.

3. **Do it for me:** business requests analysis and another team does it for them. The outputs produced would be self-served but the creation of them is not self-serve at all.

The beauty of understanding these modes is that it does not need to be one size fits all in your organisation – self-service or no self-service. You can make that decision based on the capability and maturity of each individual or team in isolation and set yourself up so that anyone can engage with data and insights in a way that suits their current or planned modus operandi. It's like at school where students learn through different approaches – text, visual, learning through play, examples, reading, watching – the ways people engage with data should be based on their preferences and/or aspirations.

This isn't really a question of self-service or no self-service but rather of deciding which is the best way to set ourselves up so that we have the best chance of making better decisions through the application and guidance of data. The decision about which mode to be in should be made in conjunction with your organisational designs and operating model that will have been set and iterated through the journey. Which team works in which mode will also change over the course of your data strategy journey and that is fine – it should be expected and planned for.

Agility × collaboration = adaptability

The traditional approaches of project management for data projects that are fixed around agreed business cases, requirements, designs and outcomes can no longer support the rapid pace of change. If we are looking to create a business that can adapt by using data and insights, we need our approach to be much more adaptable, agile and collaborative.

The shift in mindset and approach from big programmes of work and projects to sharp, outcome-focused development of data products is consistently proved to scale better and at the right pace, deliver quicker results and increase collaboration between data and business functions. We need to move from a project-centric approach to a product-centric approach.

Earlier we defined product management as the practice of strategically driving the development, launch and continual support and improvement of your organisation's data products. We defined a data product as a finished good that exists to solve a customer need, has features and KPIs and is iterated and managed by a product manager. Get used to these terms and think about how they can be applied to your business, as they help to think about your outcomes and approach to delivering those outcomes differently.

Improving data products should be an 'always on' activity, not a one-off development project that then moves to pure support mode. This may change the way you fund the development of solutions, which is typically a lump of capital expenditure (CAPEX) and then a smaller operating expenditure (OPEX) for several years. That CAPEX investment may be smaller and run for longer as you build and iterate your data products, or you may switch to a pure OPEX model to continually fund the creation of value.

This product-centric approach to data relies heavily on a huge increase in cooperation and collaboration through cross-functional teams that can work together to achieve an outcome and then continue to do so to iterate the product further. We have summarised the differences between cooperation and collaboration in the table below.

The difference is important. If everything is done with collaboration then you run the risk of an echo chamber, limited diversity in thinking and lack of creativity. If everything is done with cooperation then you may find that people go off in different directions, cracks appear and ultimately discord emerges between the teams that are allegedly cooperating.

While each on their own is important, to really drive value we need to focus on creating a culture of collaboration and cooperation between individuals, teams and organisations. This is a fundamental cultural norm that is required to be successful with data in your organisation.

Cooperation	Collaboration
Mutual respect	Mutual trust
Transparency	Vulnerability
Shared goals	Shared values
Independent	Interdependent
Short term	Long term
Sharing ideas from individuals	Generating ideas together

Set up team for scaling

We have discussed the need to think about data in terms of products and services. For these to be created and implemented, you will need people with the right capabilities. We have grouped together data jobs to allow you to start thinking about capabilities. They provide a great guideline for thinking about what type of capabilities you have and what you may need to obtain (if training existing employees is not feasible).

Depending on the priorities in your organisation, you may not need all the capabilities immediately. The best example of this is hiring a data scientist. Unless you have robust reusable data sets, have ownership in place and are progressively using a consistent approach to data management, the hiring of a data scientist is probably not your highest priority. You may hire one or two if you have budget to understand the issues you need to resolve if you want to scale, but it will be more important to ensure you have a data engineer to support their work or make it clear they need to be a generalist.

In building and scaling a data function it is useful to think about the capabilities needed by creating a job family, subfamily and jobs. A job family is a way of grouping jobs with similar characteristics, in this case data. The list of subfamily jobs below is the next level of detail. Think of a job family as a competency. You will then need to build specific jobs for each subjob family. Below is a list of the key subjob families you can begin with. By using this structure you will be able to provide good career progression to your employees and look at development plans where employees may wish to change speciality or enhance their overall knowledge. By completing this review it becomes obvious where you have gaps and when you are not immediately hiring you can look at training talent.

Initially you will want to hire people who are generalists and can do more than one competency or job. In previous organisations we have looked at each individual and assigned them up to three competencies or jobs. For example, one person could have data management, data modelling and data quality. This does not mean assigning everyone more than one competency or job. It allows you to understand your existing workforce, plan training, look at cross-fertilisation or understand coverage. It also helps you understand where your immediate hiring need is. We have always found it useful to start small and hire on a 'just in time' basis. This may sound risky but bringing on board many new hires is time-consuming and can distract from execution. The balance is an art, not a science. The key is to ensure you have a clear roadmap of MVPs in place to determine which services and products are needed and when they will be delivered. This way you can ensure that you have the right resources. It is important to make sure you don't have too many activities happening concurrently if the team does not have the bandwidth to cope.

In our experience, focusing on something that does not need tools or IT is a good place to start. On this basis we usually begin with running workshops to engage with key business stakeholders where you can share the message about change, data standards and the rest of your strategy. Your stakeholders should come out of the first session understanding that this is not just a 'data' thing but something that will fundamentally change the way the business needs to adapt.

If the workshop was focused on data ownership, for example, you could run through the following method:

- Map a customer journey / process (or confirm if work has already been completed)

- Look at one key report or metric and consider data that might be critical

- Identify issues with current process including data

- Identify where more detailed process review is needed

- Capture transformations of critical data and record high-level definitions and formulas

- Ensure the consistent data management approach and the role of the business are clearly understood

In this ownership example, identifying critical data is important as it helps people understand you won't be tackling all the data. If you are going to scale at pace, you need to make sure your first activity sets the scene. Scaling ownership means that you will need to train people on running a workshop and have in place tools for managing the content created. This includes process, policies (which should already exist), data attributes, definitions, systems and reports aligned to the business outcome you map. Ideally you should also have your data quality services fully operational, so that you are adding real value to the operational processes. The key for scaling is to ensure that you have the right data services and products ready. Any supporting services or products that may become a dependency should also have clear timeframes for completion. Be pragmatic, efficient and adaptable and ensure you adopt the start-up 'test and learn' approach.

Having people with existing skills is great but if they are not adaptable and willing to learn and change then you need to look at your bench. For example, you need someone who is familiar with data management tools and practices. This individual should be a conduit for ownership workshop training and be able to work with other data teams. If you are to scale successfully, you will need people who can develop and manage relationships outside the data teams. Your people will also need to accept that they are there to make the business look good and to be enablers for others' success. It is important to create a team mentality through your actions. For example, if your data scientist who is also doing the data engineering work is not comfortable with business or others outside data then buddy them up or, as a data leader, ensure you take the slack. If your data management expert is introverted, make sure you provide the support and mentoring to put them on an upward trajectory or buddy them with someone who is comfortable in a role where challenge and push-back are the norm.

It is important to understand what your 'keep the lights on' team looks like. You may have budget and everything in place to scale, but you need to know how you will scale back if there are circumstances that change the status quo. We have seen and worked in organisations where scaling was undertaken with no real cross-coordination and over time people, processes and systems developed on their own. Imagine an ecosystem where you did not understand the dependencies and the impact of not maintaining equilibrium. It would become unbalanced and unsustainable. Business is exactly like this if you don't manage the costs, people and processes. Evolution does not always mean scale. It does mean change. It is critical to ensure you understand how you would declutter your team and operate at minimum capacity to keep the business running.

Taking a step back and looking at the 'keep the lights on' team can also provide a fresh perspective and high-light inefficiencies. No one is above coasting when things are going great. Being prepared for the down times is easier if you understand the people, systems and process dependencies. The consistent approach to data management provides the information on what and how you transact. Undertaking regular assessments on capabilities or people, tools and processes allows you to scale effectively and declutter if cost reduction becomes a priority. This also assists with re-engineering and simplification of your organisation.

Don't scale in isolation. Data should be used to connect and drive understanding of how your organisation transacts. Scaling is not just about you and your team; it is about balance and timing. As a leader you need to be the conduit for change and be the pragmatist in the room when others are acting in a selfish and unproductive manner. This is probably the hardest skill to develop. Try thinking: 'Is this best for my customer?' first, organisational objectives second and your team last. Finally, always use the test and learn approach. In a fast-changing environment, you will need to be adaptive and move in line with both your internal ecosystem and the environment in which it operates.

The table below summarises the key roles split by disciplines. The exact titles and role definitions should be tailored to your individual organisation but it's important that disciplines and roles are covered, based on the stage of your journey.

Discipline	Role	Role summary
Leadership	Chief data officer (or senior data leader)	Leader for data. Generalist with good communication and problem-solving skills. Breaks organisational silos. May sit on the board.
Business discovery	Product manager	Responsible for the direction-setting and tracking of the roadmap for data products, plus leads the products themselves.
	Systems analyst	Technical understanding of the systems and platforms; helps ensure this is represented in data products and solutions.
	Process analyst	Specialism is the ability to manage and document process. This should also include the ability to track data flows aligned to process.
	Business analyst	An all-encompassing role that undertakes system, process and data analysis to help shape data products.
	Business engagement lead	Tracks and manages the value for data-related activity. Relationship role working closely with business stakeholders to help ensure value realisation.

Discipline	Role	Role summary
Delivery	Solution architect	Designs end-to-end and integrated data platforms that form the basis of all data work within an organisation.
	Data architect	Creates data models and related schemas. Purpose is to drive better information through reusable data sets.
	Data engineer	Designs and builds data pipelines to extract and transform a wide range of data sets.
	Software engineer	Specialist developer in big data tools and languages to build data pipelines, automations and advanced data processing.
	AI/ML engineer	An engineer who manages and monitors artificial intelligence and machine learning models in production environments.
	DataOps engineer	Focused on enabling the rapid delivery of quality data products. Responsible for the set-up of and adherence to an end-to-end tool chain that allows for process control and automation across the data value chain.

Discipline	Role	Role summary
Delivery	Data scientist	Responsible for deriving insights by using scientific methods, processes and algorithms to solve business challenges.
	Business intelligence developer	Responsible for creating reports and dashboards for others to consume.
	Analyst	Creates reports, dashboards and new analysis to help make business decisions.
Data management	Data value management manager	Responsible for setting the policies, standards and assuring best practice data management and governance approaches. Also tracks and measures value extracted from data activity.
	Data quality manager	Specialist in configurating data quality tools and assisting the business in using them.
	Data security manager	Ensures data is secure and access controlled to enable and manage risks associated with managing data.

From rigid to cross-functional organisational design

Traditional organisational structures – with rigid roles and responsibilities, boundaries around what teams can and can't get involved with, putting people, skills or teams in pigeon-holes and assuming they are unable to contribute to an agenda outside of their core skillset – hinder rather than enable you to develop an adaptable strategy and business.

Prior to the Scale stage, what's really needed is small, focused, autonomous squads that are able to apply their full attention to proving value, building credibility and delivering outcomes. If successful, this can lay the path for sticking to that kind of approach to the delivery and evolution of your data strategy.

When scaling we need to think about how we roll this concept up and out to ensure the organisation can maximise data and the outcomes it can achieve. We need to determine the best structure that allows for devolved decision-making based on quality insights. To do that we need to focus the right people and skills at the right business challenges and opportunities.

It's therefore time to move away from restricting ourselves around teams based on functional roles or capabilities. Often you will have data engineers in one team (eg IT), data scientists in another team (eg marketing), analysts in another team (eg business intelligence team in finance) and those making the changes in a business unit (eg operations). Data solutions are built by passing the baton from one team to the next, each only concerning themselves with their functional skill and part of the process. Each of these teams will be measuring themselves on completion and quality of their technical process and not on the end goal of improving an outcome for the business.

This creates bottlenecks, silos, management overhead to coordinate across the teams, lack of clarity on where issues have occurred and why, and increased importance of up-front documentation and specifications to ensure each team knows their responsibilities. This leads to inefficient delivery and reduction in pace. The result? Limited business value, missed opportunities and questions from the board about what happened to all the great ideas and investment for a better tomorrow that never arrived.

The Spotify model was introduced to the world in 2012 by Henrik Kniberg and Anders Ivarsson. It is a people-driven, autonomous approach to scaling that emphasises the importance of culture and network. They do this by focusing on autonomy, communication, accountability and quality. At the time, this was a radical approach but it helped them and other organisations increase their level of innovation and productivity. Since then this approach has been the bedrock of agile digital transformations and how Spotify scales its product development and business.

Much has been written about the pros and cons of this method; copying it to the letter is not always the best approach, but there is much to learn from it.

In the data world this approach is in its infancy, but it is already proving to be a big differentiator in building an adaptable organisation that can rapidly build, deploy and get value from data products. We need to take the approach to building a data product shown during the Prove Value stage: cross-functional, multidisciplined teams (or squads) set up to focus on an outcome and apply that to all the data products we want to build and outcomes we want to create. Even though the squads should focus on outcomes, it is important that specialists within that squad (such as data engineers, data scientists and analysts) align and collaborate on best practices to ensure consistency and high levels of quality in that discipline. You can do this by forming capability hubs, typically led by a senior specialist who is responsible for setting standards, defining best practice and assuring adherence to that.

All that said, it would be naïve to believe that this level of cross-functional collaboration, hierarchy flattening and flexibility is easy to achieve in an established business. For many this requires a transformational shift in culture and mindset in how teams work together and projects are delivered. Not all businesses have a culture that can easily pivot to this approach. We can't all behave like a start-up and it's difficult to let go of current models. On the way to this new way of working you may need to make some iterations (fix one, fix two, fix three and so on) as you move towards that goal.

In the meantime (or alongside the concepts shown above), there are three recommended approaches to how you organise the teams and capabilities in your organisation:

1. **Centralised:** bring all the 'data skills' inside your organisation into a central team who manage and deliver all the data work required, working closely with those that need it. This can be a great model for organisations looking to get control, consistency, best practice, alignment and increased quality to the data work they are doing. But this model has the potential to create an organisational bottleneck as all requirements and requests go through a single team.

2. **Distributed:** skills are spread across the organisation in different departments, geographies and business units who build their own capability and focus on their own outcomes. This is a good model for those in global and siloed businesses and often where there are multiple P&L responsibilities and therefore limited sharing of resource. The 'watch out' is that there can be high levels of duplication, limited efficiency in capability and technology investments and lack of coordination on business priorities and focus.

3. **Hybrid:** in this model (often called 'hub and spoke') there are elements of centralisation through the creation of a central 'hub' and elements of distribution through the creation of 'spokes'. The role of the hub is to set and manage the strategic direction for data and to support the spokes with tools, standards and ways of working while also providing thought leadership and insight. It must focus on delivering value and prioritisation of resources to deliver this change. The spokes' role is to focus on the needs of the business unit they are serving. They will continue to focus on their local needs but will work to the standards provided by the hub.

All of these models can work and all have challenges. None are right or wrong and effectiveness can often come down to your start point, implementation success, culture and timing. All the models need skills, clarity, education, processes and collaboration. There is a line from very centralised to very distributed and you will need to work out where is best on that line for you, now and in the future.

Whichever model you choose, we urge you to use the squads approach to ensure cross-functional, outcome-focused teams working to solve real business problems. It is also necessary to engender a culture of collaboration and cooperation to achieve maximum value from these structures.

Value-driven prioritisation

Steve Jobs famously said, 'Deciding what not to do is as important as deciding what to do.'[24] It's hard turning what look like good ideas down – it's a skill and it requires a process and practice. To achieve the level of collaboration, cooperation and focus on outcomes defined in the previous section, we need to improve how we prioritise the work that is (and isn't) done. Focusing on priority outcomes helps us be clear about what we're trying to achieve and keeps us doing the things that add value.

As a noun, 'value' is 'the regard that something is held to deserve; the importance, worth or usefulness of something', for example, 'the support you gave me was of great value'. As a verb, value means to estimate or calculate the monetary worth of something, for example, 'That data product is valued at £100,000 to our company.'[25] Both these definitions hold true when discussing data in an organisation as it can strongly value the people who contribute to the improvements of a business and apply a monetary value to what it is doing. From a prioritisation perspective it is important that both are taken into account. We value the opinions of people and what the data is saying but also the monetary return we think we will (or would

---

24 W Isaacson, 'The real leadership lessons of Steve Jobs', *Harvard Business Review*, 2012, https://hbr.org/2012/04/the-real-leadership-lessons-of-steve-jobs.

25 Definition of 'value', Oxford English Dictionary, www.lexico.com/definition/value

like to) get. This is why it can be challenging to make priority decisions in an organisation.

Have you heard of the HiPPO theory? You are in a meeting with a bunch of your directors, discussing the options for European expansion. The countries you could start with, the product market fit in different areas, the local cultures to consider, whether the marketing metrics you use in your country will work across Europe. You're making good progress, unpicking the options, considering the data, discussing the bets and close to finalising when a senior director comes into the meeting and explains which country they have decided to launch in the following financial year. Job done, decision made and what they say goes. Does this sound familiar?

HiPPO stands for the 'highest paid person's opinion' and the theory goes that the opinion of the person who is paid the most or is most senior holds more weight than others. Their opinion is often the one that gets taken forward, even in situations where this may not be the right choice. The HiPPO theory describes an organisation's reliance on the instinct of humans rather than data in the decision-making process. This is essentially the anti-approach to the whole ethos of creating a data-guided organisation.

Value-driven prioritisation is an approach that allows you to quickly measure an investment, a project, a change or an idea against the alternatives (including 'do nothing') and assess it against the overarching objectives of the organisation. It's based on the idea that we want to be working on the things that we know add most value, the biggest trusted wins, and avoid the things that drain cost, take uncalculated risks and aren't based on an objective assessment of potential (or known) upside. Sounds obvious but many organisations still don't assess the investments they make in this way. We're talking about creating a business that is guided by data; this starts with having a data-guided approach to prioritisation.

We need a mechanism for assessing value and for assessing priority based on that value. There are many different best practice models that exist for this such as RICE (reach, impact, confidence, effort), value vs effort, the MoSCoW method (must, should, could, would) and so on. Any of these can work if implemented well but the one we like that is pragmatic, simple to understand and easy to carry out is a 'business value vs ability to execute' matrix that compares how much value a product, project or outcome can deliver against an organisation's ability to deliver on it (feasibility) based on available funds, skills, technology, data, appetite and so on.

As shown in the diagram below, the items that are high value and high feasibility should be a priority. For the ones with high value and low feasibility, we should consider carrying out tests that validate the value and show whether we can improve the ability to execute. Those items that are low value and low ability to execute we want to avoid, but those that are low value but feasible we should consider closely and proceed with caution. The sum of many of those may equal more than any individual item.

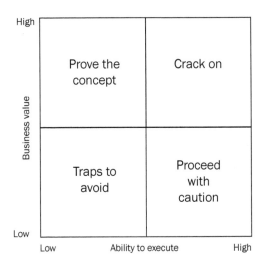

Value to feasibility prioritisation matrix

We won't always have all the information required to know if an activity is going to generate value. How can we? Yet many organisations still require detailed business cases to be drawn up with expected returns over multiple years and payback periods ahead of investing in a new idea, initiative or strategy. That's why we recommend starting with a proof of concept, test or minimum viable version of a solution with a small investment, relative to the overall potential investment. This way you can test the idea – see if it adds value, solves the problem you expected it to, works in the way you wanted it to work – and then scale it incrementally and iteratively based on the success or failure of what you try. Then you have data to make a decision about what to prioritise for further investment and what it's worth your teams focusing on. Use the data to drive both the prioritisation and the features you build into the data product.

To do this practically you need to start with a list (or backlog) of outcomes, use cases or products that you think you could work on. Earlier in the Level Up Framework we talked about capturing and documenting the use cases across your organisation. That was to help ensure that the full value chain of the business is considered so that you can assess the most valuable thing to work on. The backlog should act as a constant work in progress, be regularly reviewed (or 'groomed') and used to help decide what to work on. This can be at business objective level, data product level or even task level within teams.

Prioritisation and the process around it needs to be flexible and agile. Things change around us that are outside our control such as regulatory changes, global crises, pandemics, key personnel changes, new business risks and so on. We need to be awake to these and able to pivot our decisions on priorities so that we are working on the things that add most value (even if that means being defensive) based on the context.

Building an adaptable data platform

During the Prove Value stage we discussed putting in place a starter technology platform that allows you to prove some value-adding use cases and build credibility. Once you hit the Scale stage you should look to iterate on that platform and build out an end-to-end ecosystem that meets your requirements and the pace of change. At this stage much of the investment of time, energy and resources is spent on building out your data platform by consolidating data sets, building data products and integrating data and data products into your organisation.

Adaptability is a common thread in scaling your data strategy and ability to deliver incremental business value. The concept of levelling up is about constantly reviewing where you are, what's ahead of you and delivering value. This adaptability in the technology space is just as vital. What you need in those early stages of the journey, versus what you need as you scale, versus what you need once you hit a fully 'on rails' data strategy is going to change. We talked earlier about the importance of aligning your data platform technology and design to your defined use cases. In reality you are not going to be able to predict everything and things will change. It would be impossible to define every use case you will ever need to deliver up front because your business is going to grow, your needs are going to adjust and the priorities will shift. You need to be in a position where your platform can adapt to that change without a total rebuild each time or needing vast investments to lift and shift from one technology to another. From a technology and design point of view you will need to be adaptable and you will need an adaptable data platform.

What do we mean by a data platform? There are data warehouses, data lakes, data management platforms, data lake houses, data marts, data stores, customer insight platforms, big data platforms and many others. The market and the industry are rife with terminology and many of these terms have differing definitions but are used interchangeably. If you ask 100 people what each term means you'll have a different response from each.

To simplify things we prefer the term data platform. We use this to mean the end-to-end ecosystem of tools, technologies and architecture required to ingest, store, manage, secure, model, interact with and use data. Within that there are individual components but to most people those components aren't important. What's important is that they have the tools required for them to deliver value to your organisation.

There is plenty of technology in the market from the established players (for example Amazon, Microsoft, Google, Tableau, IBM, Informatica) to the newer entrants making a splash (Snowflake, DataRobot, Looker) to the start-ups trying to gain traction. Looking at the marketing it can be confusing to understand what part of the data ecosystem the technologies fit into and they all end up sounding the same. It's important to properly understand what you need at this stage of the Level Up Framework and what technology gaps you need to plug to satisfy your objectives. Go looking for vendors and technology solutions that fit one or more of your needs and that are aligned to your overall technology strategy.

There are six key themes to consider to ensure your data platform is adaptable.

1. Scalable architecture

You will want an architecture that allows you to start small, think and plan big and add capabilities over time in a way that doesn't back you into a corner. The architecture will need to cover the ingestion of data sets in batch and/or real time; the storage of data at various levels of consolidation, aggregation and modelling; the governance of the data platform for security, access controls, and management; and the usage and exploitation of data through analysis, reporting, further system integration and provisioning of that data elsewhere.

We discussed those components during the Prove Value stage and that had scalability built into the thinking. At that stage it was about having a light-weight platform that enabled you to deliver initial data products to prove a concept and show value.

Now we need to think about tightening up the decisions on technology and progressing the technology strategy so that you can add components as you need to, to prepare for the evolution and delivery of the required data products and services.

By knowing what's coming in terms of needs, you are able to make better decisions on what technology is needed, in what order and so that you don't end up with a Frankenstein's monster of a platform that has been built iteratively by adding new components that don't fit together in the most architecturally sound and scalable way.

Cloud platforms have a huge part to play here. In reality this technology and the reduction in cost of storage has been the accelerant to creating agile and scalable architectures at an affordable price point. Cloud should certainly form part of your thinking and plans. Some are hesitant due to concerns about privacy and ownership, so education is needed to enable organisations to utilise cloud effectively and in confidence. Moving to cloud will improve your ability to start small and scale along with your appetite and success.

2. Fit for purpose data modelling

We are at a pivotal point in design and modelling methodologies. Technologies and platforms have moved on so greatly that the constraints that traditional data modelling techniques (such as Inmon and Kimball) were designed to avoid, for example storage and computing power, are either no longer constraints or the impact has been massively reduced.

These methodologies were designed through the 1980s and 1990s and widely adopted through the 2000s. They were hugely successful and are still used today but are no longer necessary in all instances for the use cases you are trying to deliver or the workloads you need to manage. Since the technology has moved on so much and we can store, manipulate and analyse data at such volumes and complexity, we need some new design principles to cater for this new world.

There is no single methodology that is the gold standard for modelling like there was back in the 1980s and 1990s. In any case, we believe that no single modelling approach is correct for everything you want to do and instead like to take a step back from those data modelling paradigms and think about design principles and the conceptual architecture against three layers.

1. **Raw:** the raw layer is where you store unadulterated raw copies of your source data. You may refer to this layer as your data lake, which is often misused as a general term for a whole data platform. This layer is not the wild west; the data has been properly and carefully ingested, filed away and catalogued so we know

what data we have, where it's from and how recent it is. This can be structured, unstructured or semistructured data from your CRM system, website, finance system, HR system and even documents, pictures, images and video. Most users of data will not need to access this layer but it is an important step in the process of managing and providing data.

2. **Base:** the base layer is where we start to think about the structure of the data so it is more suited for presentation to analysts, dashboarding tools, data scientists and so on. We need to think here about how we design data models so they are suitable for consumption and not just broadly storage as they are in the raw layer. Here we start to consolidate data sets and apply business rules, logic, calculations, aggregations and cleansing to create an end product for the purposes of analysis. It is where your regular metrics are stored so you can report on them easily; it will allow you to answer business questions such as, 'How much revenue did we make in the Europe region last week?' or 'What was the top-ranking product in Customer A over the last twelve months compared to the previous twelve months?'

3. **Analytics:** the analytics layer is where analytical models are built and/or stored. For example, a predictive score based on certain customer attributes, a next best action model, a marketing attribution model or a demand plan algorithm.

It can also be used for simplifications of the data and data models in the base layer to, for example, provide a dashboard tool that provides self-service reporting capability to the finance department covering just the data sets that are relevant to them. It's about creating specific data outputs to suit specific business needs.

The modelling methodology used across these layers varies as the use case for each layer is different. The key tenets of the modelling you choose should be (1) optimise for the technology and platform you are using and (2) optimise for your user and your use case. These will give you the starting point for deciding the best way to store and access that data and the best way to model to suit the purpose. The way someone in the accounts payable team needs data shared with them will be different from the way a data scientist needs that same data, as their interactions and needs are different.

3. DataOps

DataOps is about applying a product management mindset to rapidly deliver (or 'ship') high-quality data products. This means moving from an idea to a data product that works and is in use quickly, then being able to iterate and improve on that product efficiently. DataOps itself is built upon three main tenets.

Firstly, it means a modern software engineering approach that takes lessons from the well-established DevOps paradigm used in the development of digital products (applications, website, apps and so on) and applies them to the way we create data products. This gives us a set of practices that work to automate and integrate the processes so we can build, test and release data products faster and more reliably. The term DevOps was formed by combining the words 'development' and 'operations' to bridge the gap between development and operations teams. DataOps is not to be confused with DevOps for data.

Secondly, it means an agile delivery methodology that provides a structure to define and implement data products iteratively and incrementally where every stage of the development process aims to add value. It brings elements of continuous improvement by measuring progress and output and finding ways to improve what you do and how you do it. We talked earlier about the ceremonies and practices that form part of this agile method and how this approach prioritises outcomes, communication, collaboration and getting work done over micromanagement, big up-front planning and working in silos.

Thirdly, it means cross-functional teams focused on valuable outcomes, which is about putting what you are trying to achieve at the heart of everything. The cross-functional element of this tells us to organise our people and teams cross-functionally, collaborating and cooperating, rather than in function or skill silos. That cross-functional team will then be centred around developing a data product that solves a specific outcome. This moves away from the traditional approach of different functional capabilities such as data engineering, dashboard development and analysts playing tag at various stages of a project, passing the baton until someone at the other end tries to deliver value. Instead all those people work in a group, obsessing about delivering the outcome together.

These three tenets make up DataOps and give us a way to create an adaptable and rapid approach to building data products and data platforms.

4. Standardisation and reusable approaches

You can move quickly, adjust quickly and be adaptable by standardising wherever possible and having reusable approaches to building your data platform. This is about having consistency on how you do things and not reinventing the wheel each time. It allows you to add new people to a team and they can hit the ground running, be productive and work in a considered and aligned way. This helps with supportability of the platform so that it's easier to unpick and fix problems if standard approaches have been used across everything. It simplifies the way you design, build and support your platform.

This should cut across: reusable data ingestion frameworks; your system configurations so you don't always need to write new code; how you handle auditing of the platform; the approach to and reporting of logging and error handling; the alerts that are produced and what information is given; and how you monitor the health of the platform and the quality of the data in there. All this should be created and managed with standardisation and reusability in mind.

There are a few layers of reusability to consider: (1) a single platform-wide way to deliver a certain activity, for example error handling always follows the same structure; (2) source type specific – the way we handle CSV files and SQL tables may be different but the concept is the same; (3) individual customisations that are specific to the problem that you are trying to solve.

5. Flexible data access

Access needs to be provided to data in numerous ways. Different people and processes within your organisation will require varying types of access to data. Some need finished dashboards with no flexibility, some need automated integrations between algorithms and customer applications, some need to be able to run their own queries and create new analysis, and some need a subset of data and to be guided around what it means. The different personas and processes drive access requirements and your approach to data access needs to be flexible.

The tools needed for each of those access approaches will differ. Unfortunately, it's not the case that you procure and implement PowerBI from Microsoft, for example, and that's all you need. That will facilitate some data access needs but not everything. It will cater for some of your reporting and dashboard needs but it won't be the best choice for real-time integrations between systems or embedded data widgets in a mobile app, for example. It will only get you so far on building data science models before you need a tool such as Alteryx or Dataiku.

Being flexible and open to different ways of providing access to data in a controlled, considered and pragmatic way will help make your data ecosystem and platform more valuable.

6. Lab and factory

The 'lab and factory' concept is sensitive to the need of organisations to balance operationally controlled and managed data environments with flexible environments that are used for experimentation and innovation. One of the things that makes a data platform adaptable is the ability to do both those things at the same time and for different people.

The lab gives you the freedom and flexibility to innovate, try new things such as test out data sets and try a new predictive model in a semigoverned environment, with a wide selection of tools available. It allows you to test and learn and only go forward with the things that add value. You can have multiple people with multiple lab environments to suit their own local needs.

The factory is an environment that is more tightly controlled by a dedicated team, with controls to govern changes, the technology that can be used and how it is accessed. It will have a more rigorous testing and validation cycle before any new products or code are released into the environment. Typically, your board, corporate or regular KPI reporting packs will come from this environment, as will any models or algorithms that are powering your marketing campaigns or personalisation on an app.

The critical element is the route you establish from the lab environment to the factory environment, often referred to as 'lab to live'. There is a danger you end up with lots of experiments all over the place and nothing working on rails, at scale or being used to improve the business, with no established route to do so. You can also inadvertently end up creating more silos, more stovepipes between people and data. It's important to agree an approach for going from lab to factory, which requires the team working together, technology to support this and processes agreed. DataOps is an approach that supports this.

This language works well across the organisation (with non-technical or data people) and it resonates as it aligns to the metaphor of a laboratory for investigation, experimentation and testing, and a factory that has a set process, control and governance and ships out consistent, quality products.

Building reusable components

Reusability is broader than just your core data platform. When building your understanding about how your organisation connects, it is important that you can record, reuse and maintain the knowledge gathered. This will require not just culture change but also a set of tools. Effectively you are recording and building the organisational ecosystem. There are three core components for success:

- **Culture change:** this happens over time through an increased understanding and management of data. It requires collaboration, communication and education, with strong leadership support. By breaking down organisation silos, data supports a customer-driven approach and starts the evolution towards being data-guided. This will require organisational change over time.

- **Consistency:** this is provided by implementing an approach for data management that is simple and pragmatic. Supporting tooling is used to ensure capture and reuse of institutional knowledge (business metadata). This also provides support for ongoing education. The data standards and knowledge capture create a broader understanding of how things connect and assist with increasing data literacy as well as overall business literacy.

- **Discovery:** through discovery, definition, understanding context, tagging, and securing data, information is improved. A consistent data management approach, tools and process understanding increase the ability of an organisation to change rapidly.

The tooling building blocks supporting data management and the relationship of these tools with the organisation's existing systems and external data sources is shown in the diagram below. The different layers highlight the dependencies when implementing tools to help build a complete picture of your organisation's ecosystem. The jigsaw pieces allow you to identify the different components that may be missing in an organisation's approach to managing data and information.

The key point here is that these parts are interdependent. The value and ability to map, understand, maintain and adapt your organisation are predicated on being able to connect and understand. The building blocks must have the capabilities defined below to enable your organisation to capture, reuse and maintain the information while implementing your ambition to be data-guided. Too often the focus is on the tools, a specific vendor or a pet project. This may be a reporting project, a traditional business glossary or even master data. You are building the data products and services to create value aligned to your business outcomes. These building blocks are a simple way to ensure you build the right products and services and understand how the capabilities create a connected data ecosystem.

It is also important to recognise that by connecting the way your organisation transacts you are also enabling regulatory compliance, should that be needed. For example if you have defined some key personal data as critical, you will apply a set of standards to manage this data. It should be tagged with various attributes which could highlight destruction dates, type of sensitivity, etc. You will have clear business definitions and be able to see where in your systems and platforms it exists. You will have data quality rules to ensure it is correct and potentially be mastering the data too. Data flow will be linked to key processes using and creating the data. In addition you will have clear ownership assigned to the process, the system the data resides in and its definitions. All these outputs are the result of building an effective data ecosystem. Regulation might mean you focus on what data is tackled first but how you do it should be driven by a need to want to connect, understand and drive innovation, agility and adaptability.

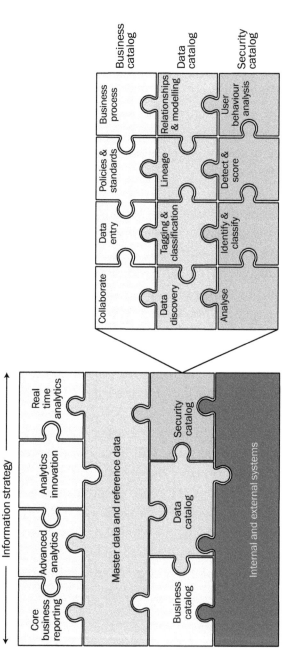

Reusable components and their interdependencies

Sorting out who owns the data

The one activity that fundamentally changes the way people think, behave and act is the implementation of a common ownership model. Ownership is a fundamental driver of change. Ownership is not just a data problem. As part of the adoption of the ownership model, it is important that ownership is applied consistently across the business. Systems, policies, data and processes all need ownership. Having ownership just for data and not the other key parts of the business won't create the momentum and collaboration needed.

For most people in most companies, you will probably agree that ownership is ambiguous. How many meetings have you been in where people have said, 'Oh, John owns this, Jill owns that'? It means nothing, and there's no way to record who owns what; there are no clear boundary conditions and no ongoing maintenance of ownership. By maintenance we mean the artefacts that ensure ownership is fit for purpose and meets business or regulatory needs.

When we began to look at ownership for data, it became apparent that we couldn't just assign ownership to data only. We added process, as this gave the context or boundary conditions. There is a requirement for ownership to be specific, to have some form of context and be framed so that it is understood by the business.

There is also a need for ownership to be maintained on an ongoing basis. This maintenance needs to be part of how the business operates. It is not about command and control. This is not data governance, this is good business. Why do we bother to assign ownership to something in an organisation? The answer is simple: if something isn't maintained and isn't fit for purpose, that presents the organisation with a risk. In most organisations this will manifest as an operational risk. However, risk generally has a wider impact; for example, if it affects customers it may cause reputational risk and if there is a large media impact it could affect the share price. We want to minimise the risk, pragmatically embedded within our data program.

If something doesn't work as intended in the organisation, it means the needs of customers, shareholders or employees are not being met. This presents an operational risk. We need to ensure that we manage and maintain ownership to mitigate or minimise risk. That's why maintenance and attestation to ensure the process and/or data are fit for purpose and makes sense. It helps drive the organisation's efficiency through documentation of how things work. It also forms part of our consistent data management approach through understanding critical data, both definitions and flows.

How do we do this? The answer is simple and may exist in your organisation. You assign ownership to the risk framework or the operational risk framework of the organisation. If your organisation doesn't have a risk framework, you can develop a simple one – creating a list of key risks and mitigating them as needed. When you map a process, you also understand the risks involved. Much like mapping the data flow, this is a new capability you need to create. This does not necessarily need new systems or teams but ideally becomes part of how you simplify and re-engineer for better customer outcomes and reducing operational risk. A key component here is to have a set of simple controls. Controls are tests you run on a regular basis. This allows you to ensure you have an owner responsible for confirming at least annually that what they own is fit for purpose. For example, if you assign ownership to a piece of process or a piece of data or a set of data, you need to know that every year, at a minimum, someone has attested to the fact that it is fit for purpose.

This is also the time to look at the effectiveness and efficiency of what is being done. This is especially true if you are implementing a more digital footprint. If it is not efficient and effective, the owners need to create an action plan to upgrade or improve or re-engineer at some point in the future. It doesn't need to be done tomorrow, but if it is not upgraded at some point it will continue to present a larger risk, and that risk needs to be mitigated.

'Accountable' and 'responsible' seem like a good place to start when looking at ownership. But accountability and responsibility by themselves are ambiguous and are often confused. To provide clarity, we add two terms: '100% committed', which in effect means no stone unturned and is the highest standard, and 'reasonable', meaning that what should be done will be done. We now have context and a way to determine at what ownership means. But while we might assign someone to be accountable for something, ownership requires collaboration. The ownership model we are providing is a shared model. This does not mean accountability is reduced; it is enhanced as the accountable individual has a clear view on the boundary conditions and who else is involved.

Let's use the example of a process that runs across an organisation. Like most processes, it involves many teams and people in different silos. We need to think about process in two ways: discrete process and end-to-end process. Discrete process is work that is undertaken by an individual or by a team, or even by a function that we can easily recognise, because it is what they do as part of their job. It's why these people, individuals or teams come to work. We are looking at the output of the teams as part of that process. If you add up these discrete processes, the result is an end-to-end process, something with a clear beginning and end. In being pragmatic, we are not looking to document a process into micro steps unless it is necessary. It may be necessary to understand a process between two points which may branch off and begin another process. Start with something manageable and easily understood. At a later point you can connect the key processes.

Let's now look at defining how the ownership model works. We will define the key terms outlined above and then apply them to some generic data roles. This provides transparency for you to think about how you can apply this to your organisation. It is not intended that you have ownership applied at a junior level in the organisation. A good rule of thumb is to apply it one or two levels below the executive.

Accountable and responsible

For simplicity, accountability and responsibility are compared to provide clarity of their use.

The main difference between responsibility and accountability is that responsibility can be shared while accountability cannot. Being accountable not only means being responsible for something but also being answerable for your actions. Accountability is something you hold a person to only after a task is done or not done. Responsibility can be before and/or after a task.

100% committed

Performing a duty on a '100% committed' basis is the onerous standard. If you are accountable or responsible for performing a duty on a 100% committed basis, this means that everything that can be done should be done. This does not mean taking actions that are not commercially efficient or effective. The phrase 'no stone unturned' exemplifies the 100% committed standard.

Reasonable effort

By contrast, 'reasonable effort' implies that what can be done should be done in the context and purpose of the duty being performed, but without the responsible or accountable party needing to leave 'no stone unturned'. 'Reasonable effort' is a less onerous standard than 100% committed.

Critical data owner

Critical data is identified through understanding the process that gives it context and makes it critical. The owner of critical data is required to ensure there is a simple definition that is maintained in the business glossary. They may also help define data quality thresholds in line with consumers and producers to ensure that the validity of data is appropriate. While there may be exceptions, assisting with data quality thresholds should be consistent. It is necessary for critical data to have both a business glossary term and data dictionary metadata.

Discrete process owner

A discrete process owner can be described as someone who undertakes a function and produces something, ie a report or output for another process. The activity is undertaken as part of the role of the individual or team. The reason discrete ownership is important is that assigning ownership on this basis is easier than trying to define an owner for end-to-end process. The approach for ownership is to identify the key process steps at a high level and assign owners to the discrete boxes.

This is shown in the figure below, where a process has been mapped with six key component parts. This process is coloured light grey. However, like data, end-to-end process is also contextual and for a particular context the process may have other activities that need to be understood. The dark grey shapes represent the other activity that needs to be brought into scope, with the arrows indicating other activity which is not yet understood.

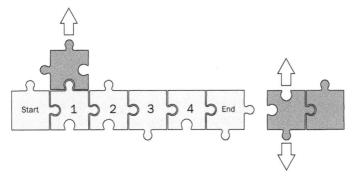

Ownership components process example

As process is joined and understood more broadly, the understanding of what happens in an organisation can be used to drive simplification and cost effectiveness. This is part of understanding the connections in your organisation, which will take time. Always start at a high level when documenting and get more detail as required. This ensures you can assign ownership quickly.

The other reason discrete ownership is important is that by understanding key breakpoints in a process and having an owner, you can assign actions where the data quality thresholds are not being met. This is a key part of the data management approach where data quality rules are run across a process.

End-to-end process owner

While you may start by mapping only start and end points based on your scope, eventually looking at end-to-end process will be required. While additional effort to map end-to-end process is required, it will likely be done as part of digitising, regulatory compliance or a re-engineering effort.

Traditionally the issue with someone being 'accountable' is the implication that they have sole accountability. It is not practical for an end-to-end owner to understand the detail of the full end-to-end process, as the process will inevitably cross multiple teams of the organisation. By having someone own the detail (responsible on a 100% committed basis) and an accountable owner on a reasonable basis, you have a working shared model. The individual is still the sole person accountable but they have a team of people to resolve issues in the process. Accountability is about managing the discrete owners.

The following conditions are provided to help ensure accountability is supported:

- The process should be documented 'end to end' to ensure that all critical steps are understood.

- If the process being documented forms part of a more complex process, the start and end points need to be clearly outlined and reference made to other key processes that are impacted.

- The business outcome and critical data need to be clearly identified in the process. The outcome of the documentation is to capture and understand the process and data and allow this 'asset' to be available in a business glossary.

- Where an existing process has been documented, it can be referenced rather than repeated.

- Sign off needs to be clearly aligned to the specific role of the individual, eg accountable on a reasonable basis.

- Data quality breakpoints need to be clearly defined to ensure that data quality rules can be run across the process. This allows for appropriate assignment to correct issues when quality thresholds are not met.

System owner (custodian)

It is important to have systems owners assigned. Technology does not own data but they need to be identified as they are an important part of maintaining good data and enabling straight-through process. They maintain the responsibility for ensuring that systems are current, working and supporting business processes. They are responsible for ensuring the system controls and systems are defined in line with business requirements on a 100% committed basis.

Data consumer

All users of data are required to understand their responsibilities in transacting process and using data. They have a responsibility on a reasonable basis for understanding their consumption of data. This is an important part of becoming a data-guided business.

Data producer

All producers of data are required to understand their impact on process and business outcomes as aligned to the data policy principles and data standards. They have accountability on a 100% committed basis for what they produce.

Data strategist

The data strategist is accountable on a 100% committed basis for ensuring the right policy, strategy and standards are available for the organisation to operate effectively, enabling its business objectives to be met.

Adaptive data management as a service

While the size and complexity of problems vary in different organisations, the core issues are the same. This means you can solve them in a consistent way. With increased experience you can develop internal capability and increase the pace of change. This also enables you to drive stability and robustness in how you look not just at data but also at business problems. By using a consistent approach to data management, you can create momentum and durability in joining data in your organisation. This approach focuses on process mapping as a starting point.

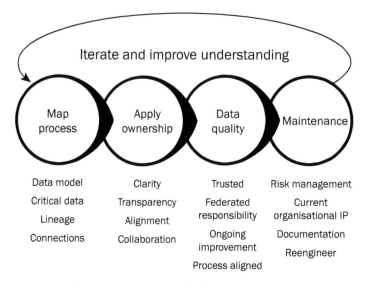

A common approach to data management

How: agility and adaptability

- Consistent approach to solving business issues
- Collaborate and break down silos
- Agility and adaptability in execution
- Data standards applied pragmatically

Why: common approach to managing and understanding data

- Reference architecture alignment
- Think differently to re-engineer mapped processes

- Transparency and connections from mapped process align to customer journeys and digital agenda

- Understand value

Who: data capability needed

- Virtual or small team (Change, IT, Business)

- Everyone responsible

- Drive accountability

- Develop organisation capability

Data needs to be embedded into your DNA and a part of how you operate. Data needs context and adaptive management based on the culture, users and business objectives. We need to build a window into the organisation that provides a way to join process, risk, policy, standards and data. This business metadata (data that provides you with information about other data) will be built over time. It will provide an understanding of how the organisation operates and allow acceleration of change. We need to move away from legacy thinking. If your business is looking to create a culture that supports efficient use and exploitation of data, you need to manage the asset you are building. The rationale for calling it a service is that you need to be able to provide specialist skills and resources to ensure the organisation not only adopts but also takes on a broader responsibility for data.

We will do this by building the data products and services to support management of data. What does managing data really mean, and why not data governance? Management is about doing. Management is about the activity of controlling something, or of using or dealing with something in an effective way. It's about taking decisions. It's about execution. If you have an asset, you need to manage that asset. There are different components to data management, but they are tightly connected. If you miss a component, it is like building a house with only three walls. We suggest using the Level Up Framework to ensure you are building the components in the right way, in the right order and at the right time.

Use the building blocks to understand the components needed for adaptive data management. The tools required for holistic data management have been defined above but even if you have unlimited resources you can't implement them all at once. This is why using a particular use case to drive a set of data products and services that are only just good enough makes sense. It is recommended that you create the tooling infrastructure you will need up front to enable you to build the right processes and understand the roadblocks, which are not always evident when planning a project. These are likely to be cultural and process barriers to getting things done differently.

Data Management

Data security	Business glossary	Data catalog	Data quality	Information delivery	Ownership	Data standards	Master data	Sunset
Access	Business meaning	Technical meaning	Profiling	Core business reporting	Risk management	Policy	Reference data	Achieve
Confidentiality	Process context	Eco-system connections	Assessment service	Advanced analytics	All organisation assets	Reference point for decisions	Hierarchies	Anonymise
Availability	Collaboration & search	Lineage	Monitoring & reconciliation	Analytics innovation	Maintenance	Fix forward	Consistency	Remove
Integrity & protection	Discovery	Classify	Remediation	Real time analytics	Control	Reference architecture	Trusted	Auditable access

Data management building blocks

The key is not to be rigid. The organisation should understand that delivery of all the data products and services cannot be done in a big bang approach. Too many data programs try to solve all problems and be all things to everyone. You don't need all your data defined in a glossary, you don't need the lineage of all processes, you just need to add value to something that is going to exist or is already underway. You also need to ensure that you reference the data standards and are not creating more legacy. To be adaptive, you need to be resilient and creative with how you solve problems. You need to bring together people who don't normally cooperate or collaborate.

Start with ownership. Ownership is fundamental to drive change and provide the governance needed. This governance is tightly coupled with your organisation's risk framework. You align ownership of process, systems, data and so on. You make sure that it's maintained and managed, and it presents no material risk to the organisation. If your data is poor, and your process is ineffective and prone to errors, then your customers won't have an optimal journey. You are effectively introducing operational risk in how you operate. Ownership is aligning governance to existing ways of working. Traditional data governance is set up for command and control. In a fast-moving ecosystem, you need to be adaptive and weave data management into everyone's role. You do this through effective ownership.

One of the things that will need ownership is critical data. This could be a term for a data attribute, a key business metric or data specific to a function that may have multiple meanings elsewhere in your organisation or wider business ecosystem. Many organisations creating a data management function start with establishing a business glossary. This is a key component but it needs to be established with ownership of process and be built incrementally. Too many organisations try to build the glossary as a stand-alone asset and try to include everything. We don't advocate this. Use start-up thinking, with an MVP approach, building the glossary alongside other key components. Good data management is about ensuring you can join the data as it is created, transformed, moved and used in multiple business contexts.

Defining something by itself has little value to the business. With ownership, understanding where the data resides in your system and applications and where it is used in process and reporting, we are building an understanding and connecting different parts of the organisation. This supports faster change and makes the information more useful to more people. It also ensures you understand how things are transacted and can prioritise improving and driving a digital agenda. All the components of data management are dependent on each other. As a collective they are powerful and will help you understand how your business operates and highlight the interdependencies. This provides a platform for transformation, digital or nondigital.

A key part of creating a data-guided organisation is to federate data services into the business process. A great place to start is data quality, a component that businesses are keen to engage with. It allows you to start getting the wider organisation to understand that data is everyone's responsibility. Data quality has subcomponents. The subcomponents are data profiling, data quality assessment, monitoring and reconciliation, and remediation. Data quality helps create trusted and clean data that can be relied on for decision-making, supporting automated decisions and in reporting. The way most people in your organisation engage with data is reporting, where poor quality is always highlighted. With the introduction of the General Data Protection Regulation (GDPR), having a set of individual customers that has been quality checked is an immediate need that allows you to show value in meeting regulatory requirements but can also add value to understanding and communicating with customers.

It is important, as you build your data management services and products, to create them based on a current business need. This could be part of a change programme, solving a BAU (business as usual) activity or simplifying current operational practices. By using this data management approach, you will produce consistent solutions that are adaptive and pragmatic. The consistent approach to data management ensures that you always understand the context for the data you are working on. By focusing on process, you can engage and start educating the wider business. In applying ownership and data quality, you are making sure that the organisation does not lose valuable insight into how a business outcome is transacted. Most importantly, you are ensuring this knowledge is maintained and can be used to support change and re-engineering for simplicity and a more digital business. However, a fundamental key for the data management service is federating the services into BAU. This increases the data competency and understanding of the business in your organisation.

Organisation evolution is about understanding how you need to manage changing the organisational construct. If you do not have a data team, is it best to create a new team or focus on creating people capability? When do you create a data function or will augmenting existing teams work better in the organisation? The key here is to understand how the culture drives activity and what has gone before you. Whatever organisational structure you start with and however you plan to create the data-guided organisation, you will need capable people. This must follow the adaptable and pragmatic approach we suggest as part of the start-up best practice.

The data function should be a small and expert group of people who support the wider business through training and helping to evolve data services. It is important that these services are not just provided by the centralised data team. Initially this is crucial, but as you mature and become a data-guided organisation, you should be developing people capability in various parts of the business through federation of the services and products. If we take the data quality example, over time you should have people in the business who can develop their own data quality rules. They should be able to run ownership workshops and undertake one-off data quality assessments. They will have a specific business lens based on their place in the organisation but as they develop, they will also be able to learn other parts of the business. By running an ownership workshop, an individual will develop an understanding of a part of the business they may know little about. This also supports innovation and collaboration.

You should have a clear understanding of what you are aiming to achieve. While a policy is important, you can start with data standards and graduate to a policy. Using fix forward and standards, you are looking to educate and change legacy behaviour that created whatever mess you have. The standards become a reference point for decision-making and allow whoever you appoint as the data leader to use these to drive change. If you have no standards and have never considered using data effectively, it is unrealistic to expect all standards to be met immediately. The key focus should be on education, increasing data understanding and ensuring that all new activity is aimed at adopting and moving towards the standards.

Being adaptive and evolving your people through the use and management of data is a key benefit of driving a better business understanding. Having tools that allow you to capture, maintain and share this information provides a way to drive collaboration and understanding. It also provides a vehicle for challenge and innovation. People who don't understand a process or the meaning of a piece of data can add value by questioning. This ensures that consistency is reached or helps develop new information to bring greater clarity to the organisation. By adopting a start-up approach, you build only what's needed. You develop products and services based on the needs of the organisation and they will be incrementally scaled and optimised. The data management service evolves and develops based on the environment in which it operates. It is crucial that the leadership in your organisation understands that setting up the right culture and infrastructure for data is fundamental to having data management that is adaptive, evolves and adds value.

Scale: the breakthrough criteria

In order to punch through to the Accelerate stage, there are some important outcomes you need to have reached so that you can ensure strong foundations are in place.

1. **Broad and deep value delivered:** the most important criterion is that you have delivered stated and articulated incremental business value through the delivery of data products. This should be across a broad range of business areas and deep in several of them.

2. **Working on the top business priorities:** the efforts of those working on data products should be focused on the top three to five business priorities.

3. **Optimum efficient organisation:** you will need all the key skills required to operate a data strategy at scale. While you may have gaps in bandwidth, you should have no major gaps in capability by the end of this stage.

4. **High demand for data products:** you should have the problem of too much demand rather than trying to create demand. The main business units, functions and teams should be represented in your backlog of use cases.

5. **Embedded collaborative and efficient ways of working:** modern software engineering approaches, agile ways of working and cross-functional teams working on a business outcome should be well embedded.

6. **Data ownership and management processes in place:** questions over data ownership and how

your core data is managed should be mostly ironed out.

7. **Investment needed for the Accelerate stage:** you need to have secured budget to move to the next stage of your journey.

8. **Your plan for the Accelerate stage:** you need a clear plan that explains what you will do through the Accelerate stage and changes that you will make.

FIVE

Accelerate

You should always be looking to move at pace but by this stage it is about accelerating at scale. That's only possible if you have scaled on solid foundations through the previous stages. Poor foundations, poor value delivery or poor team organisation mean you cannot move fast or effectively. At this stage it's about accelerated decision-making. That comes from an understanding that:

- Insights are more valuable the sooner they can be acted upon.

- Insights should be integrated directly into other applications and business processes.

- The insights we want to identify are complex and real-time.

To accelerate at scale

The points we have made around building data services and products and federating them into the organisation using an iterative approach are not just about building capabilities. They are there to ensure that as your organisation adopts the change you are building, it accepts that data is everyone's responsibility and that this is about being able to make more decisions more often so that you can get things right for your organisation and its customers.

An ecosystem is complex and will always change because of internal and external influences. You may be accelerating different parts of the data estate based on your organisational needs but you must understand that scaling other components requires scaling at pace. It is important that this does not become a 'technology or tools' project.

Let's use AI models as an example. Creating an AI model will require specialists in the data organisation, collaboration with IT to build the right data pipelines and information security to ensure only the right people have access to data, and working with your data protection officer and product teams to ensure GDPR requirements are followed. The complexity cannot be ignored. We must ensure we have a clear rationale for the model. Its purpose is to speed up part of a customer journey by automating a decision.

If we follow the approach outlined, we will have established all the data services and products needed. When undertaking the various MVPs to prove we have all the necessary components, we should also understand how to extract and measure value. It is critical that you ensure the organisation is ready to change. If you have not considered the impact of the model to the operational processes, implementing a model will be difficult. The model will not be static so establishing relevant processes to manage and update the model as part of BAU is also required (often referred to as model management). Once this has been done, you can use the test and learn approach to hone your implementation process. Now you have a model in BAU, what next?

This creates a conundrum for a lot of organisations. How do you invest in the change necessary to accelerate? Do you create a new organisation in tandem with running down the legacy? Where to start? Part of the answer lies in selecting the right team. If you have analysed the people you have, started upskilling or hired the skills you don't have, then you are part way there. In scale you should have created the organisation, processes and products and services needed. If you haven't, then you are not ready to optimise. Let's assume this has been done; you should have implemented a number of data products and services multiple times. In each iteration of the implementation, you should learn how to make the processes more robust and automated.

Accelerating is not just about automation and creating straight-through processing. It is also about creating detailed event-driven measurement. The ontology you developed will be maturing as you scale and understand the events you want to measure and how they relate to your customers or your internal organisation. This understanding brings the need for new metrics, more sophisticated analysis of data relationships and more data. You are now looking to automate, simplify and create a deeper understanding of how your organisation works and delivers to your customers. What your customers want and how they want it should also be a targeted outcome.

Technology enablement

We talked earlier about creating all the technology components needed to scale. These were broken down to allow for the necessary data products and services to be aligned to business objectives. This assisted with planning what and when to create the infrastructure you needed to scale. If you have not created the components with the adaptability lens, then acceleration is not impossible but will be more expensive and take longer. The ability to build reusable and scalable components in the cloud makes this easier. Synchronisation of multiple cloud environments from different vendors, reducing reliance on one vendor or trying to only build open source all present issues that need to be managed.

Ensuring that the IT function understands the roadmap and functionality is critical. Many organisations forget that your technology stack is not forever. In building the components, you need to think like your team: 'What's the "keep the lights on" stack and what do I need to build now to ensure I can migrate off a vendor to another vendor or open-source application?' The technology stack will be continually evolving but at a pace that is cost effective and in line with other change.

Don't fall into the technology trap. There is never a single technology that solves everything but if you scaled correctly, you may need to accept that payback on that investment means not upgrading your technology as often as you might like. There is always a place for innovation but if your organisation thinks that X is the silver bullet needed to go to the next level, then make sure you have thought about all the people, processes and change that is needed. Too often organisations assume that changing their technology will solve their problems, and the speed to delivery is undertaken without considering the broader organisation and environmental ecosystem.

DataOps and automation

We have espoused the value of utilising process or customer journeys to understand data better and connect it to how you transact, while managing risk. The principles of collaboration, simplification and automation should now be second nature. To fully optimise, you have built the right products and services needed for delivery. Ownership is in place and activity is federated throughout your organisation. What is needed to take you to the next level?

The connection of your data products and services to the wider organisation and their delivery needs an effective approach. DataOps is an automated, process-oriented methodology. The focus is primarily on data and analytic and data teams. The objective is to improve the quality and reduce the cycle time of data analytics. We take a broader view and are looking to create collaboration across the data lifecycle for all data, business, risk, operational and technology teams. This is not to be confused with the Agile approach to working. While using the Agile methodology to shorten the cycle time of analytics development is important, flexibility and adaptability in using these methodologies is needed. Six Sigma is a detailed and mathematical approach to process efficiency. Project management has been codified and there are standards on good project management. However, while both these approaches have value, they can also produce massive inefficiencies if used incorrectly.

Common sense, good leadership and the ability to make decisions are key. As long as you apply the test and learn philosophy, you should be able to move forward. While DataOps has borrowed some of the principles and practices around continuous delivery and automated testing that were matured by DevOps, simply applying DevOps to data is not enough. DataOps utilises statistical process control (SPC) to monitor and control the data analytics pipeline, ensuring that data is constantly monitored and managed. We have discussed the need to build people and process to monitor analytical models in production. SPC is a part of that process. DataOps is not tied to a particular architecture, toolset or technology. The Level Up Framework is a common-sense approach to drive a change in thinking. The consistent approach to data management is there to promote collaboration, optimise your organisation, improve process and data quality, and manage security, access and ease of use of data.

Automation to reduce cycle times and continually improve the data pipelines feeding analytical models and information delivery should be continuous. This includes fully utilising event data and driving automation into all processes. The introduction of more detailed triggers in process allows for automation of metrics to drive compliance with internal or external service level agreements. This is not without a cost. There will be legacy to decommission and you must bring your people along. The approach at this stage should be focused on automating everything you can. Make it as hands-free as possible and allow your valuable human resources to focus on true value-adding and decision-making activities.

Refresh your organisation

Organisational change is hard. It sucks when you need to let good people go because they won't or can't change in line with the new way of operating, but it is necessary. The change needed is not just a data thing. Process changes will be needed to digitise the inputs captured when transacting. The skills of people in the organisation will change and need to be developed to create a more flexible and adaptable workforce. Like data, strategic workforce planning is an organisational need and should be adopted by the entire organisation. There is a fear that AI will destroy jobs but it also presents opportunities to create new jobs throughout the organisation. It is optimal to keep internal knowledge about how an organisation works, so cultivating your existing workforce is always preferable.

Job families, position management, clear business hierarchies, current and maintained line management hierarchies are just some of the data inputs needed. It is important that you don't just focus on customer activity; you need to consider all the foundational capabilities. The good news is that this is not a zero sum game. Improving your basic reporting capability to have more reusable data sets needs some basic components, for example good finance data that can be linked to your employee population and sales data. An understanding of the cost of the entire organisation by geography, product and structure is needed to run an efficient business. It's important to start this at the beginning of the Prove Value phase.

How has the culture changed?

You may have a crack team and all the tools you need to capture knowledge, manage how you transact and keep ahead of regulatory questions, but if your culture has not evolved then you are not ready to accelerate. How do you know your organisation has maintained the culture change? Endless budget and little questioning on what it is being spent on sounds good but is it really where you want to be? The last thing you want is to accelerate when you are over-confident and not maintaining the pragmatism and adaptability that are vital for initial and ongoing success. What does success look like?

The data team is everyone in the organisation. By the time you are ready to optimise, you should have built not only the right tools but also the right people. Your culture is not all about data, it is just the way you operate. It is part of the ecosystem; we don't think about it but understand its inherent value. The capture of how you operate is federated and the tools are part of the organisational fabric. Innovation and adaptability are key tenets of your culture and there is less silo thinking with more cooperation and collaboration. These things are not necessarily everywhere in the organisation but they are the norm. It is easy to take this all for granted but pragmatism, collaboration and pace will need to be refined and maintained. As your organisation and the wider world evolve and change, the things you do to keep this culture also need to mature.

Federated data knowledge

As you develop a deeper understanding of how you operate by capturing events and semistructured data from a multitude of sources, you need to be able to manage, understand and use this data. We have all heard of the data swamp. This is a good sign you have leapt from establishing to scaling/optimising before proving value. It is likely that, having done this, you have not built the data products and services needed to support this increase in data capture. By taking a pragmatic and measured approach, you can make the right gains and make them sustainable. Often organisations accelerate parts of the data infrastructure and have to go back and start building what they neglected because it was not in vogue. If you don't have good data management fundamentals in place, the scope of the project exponentially grows and it can fail.

However, if you build the components in a measured way and federate the use of the products in your organisation, you provide a way to improve operational process, upskill your people and start building a culture that accepts data has value. But knowing value is there is not enough. When people adopt new ways of working, the value is evident in how effectively inefficient activity is reduced or how the role is materially changed. A key success factor for understanding if your organisation has made the transition culturally is the push for more data change; there should be pressure to increase the scale and optimisation of the change already undertaken.

It is not just data tools that are federated. APIs that are available for all to understand in your data and business catalogues, microservices delivering a fully integrated data platform and linking everything your organisation does, automated decisions and straight-through processing – these are all signs you are ready to optimise.

Monetising data externally

It's important to measure value from the start. At this stage you are not ready to think about how to monetise the data. Let's think about this from an internal perspective first. There is value in understanding which products and customers provide the greatest margin and which products have purely symbiotic value, whereby they are needed for other products to succeed or be a feeder for other products. Increasing cross-sell and better understating lifetime value and key events in the customer journeys in your organisation or customers' key life events also have internal value.

It is important to consider the value of capturing, maintaining and managing how you transact but measuring the value is not easy. Often you save parts of jobs. If you have no way of understanding how this adds value and have decided at what point organisational structure change is needed, then you will only ever have numbers on a spreadsheet. The independencies are obvious. If you understand the skills you need and what the organisation needs to look like, you are managing the risk through clear ownership, and you are continually commoditising your approach to data, change and creating a better customer experience – all these things by themselves are powerful but when done in a considered way provide exponential returns. What about external value?

Now that you understand what data you have, you can quickly define and create relationships, manage and use data, then you can look at selling this to others who have not made the development you have. Think about the data products and services we have built. We can now record who consents to their data being used for multiple purposes, and we understand who and what the customer wants by building a picture through data. Selling data externally is not just about bundling it up and pushing it out the door. If we sell data, it needs to be in line with our ethics and values. Too often organisations rush to find the silver bullet but don't understand the complexities of where they operate internally or externally. There is value in data but it cannot be achieved by looking at and managing data in a silo; you must track and understand value from the beginning. Don't try to make data the star – it is an enabler. There is incredible value in having conversations about what part data has in increasing customer penetration or what can be done with better information or automating a decision or digitising a process.

There is also the option of selling the data you have to others but doing this too early in the process creates risk. Not only external reputational risk to partners, customers and regulators but internal risk through inefficient delivery. Much like trying to implement master data management before you have the data management fundamentals in place, if you sell your data too early you increase the scope of what's needed to do this properly and efficiently. Selling more to existing customers, faster and with better products is a far better goal to have. It improves the core business and ensures that you control costs and automate where possible. Selling your data to other parties is certainly an option but one that needs to be considered properly. Ignore the hype and focus on good data and business fundamentals.

Accelerate: the breakthrough criteria

To punch through to the Optimise stage there are some important outcomes you need to have reached to ensure strong foundations are in place.

1. **Value alignment:** the organisation now has a clear proxy or set of metrics that are used as part of the planning process. Value is measured and calculated robustly, not made up or slashed to meet a target.

2. **Data-guided:** the organisation is now mature in its thinking about data and its part in success. There are no debates about 'why' and data is what the organisation focuses on.

3. **Data and business strategy aligned:** there is no longer a data strategy; the business strategy and the plan to implement it are amalgamated. Process work is synonymous with data flows and digital enablement. The strategy is connected and focused.

4. **Prioritisation pragmatism:** the silos in the organisation are weak and there is clarity on what takes priority. Change is managed in a mature and logical manner. There are clear plans and an understanding of the independencies that exist for the change to be executed.

5. **Organisational agility:** the capability of people can be utilised effectively. This could mean cross-

functional teams, scaled agility or whatever works in your organisation. It does not need to include by-the-book methodologies.

6. **People capability:** the right balance of buying in or building capability is in place. This forms a key part of the employee experience and is a foundation of the culture. Employees are challenged to develop in line with the organisation's needs.

7. **Ecosystem clarity:** you have connected and continually re-engineered how things are done to embed straight-through processing, AI automation and robotics process automation. This simplifies what is done and ensures that data can be gathered to continually adapt as stream analytics continues to build the view on how you transact.

8. **Technology is effective and flexible:** technology has matured to create the right platform for innovation and fine-tuning data flows, integration of AI models and development of new data products to meet business needs.

SIX

Optimise

Over the last decade more and more digital-only businesses have been created and businesses with a physical foundation have invested in digital transformation. Those that succeed have used technology to change how they interact with their customers, manage their processes and think about innovation. The Optimise stage is reserved for the few that can behave like digital natives and big technology organisations leading the charge.

Introducing the data native

Some of the biggest tech giants such as Facebook, Amazon, Google, Uber, Netflix, Apple and Spotify have built products and services that are underpinned by data and moved beyond the product and service we as consumers engage with. Their product is really their data and their technology platform.

In the UK, Gousto was recently valued at more than $1 billion, one of only a few businesses to do this in the food and drink sector. Gousto supplies subscribers with recipe kit boxes including everything you need to cook individual and easy-to-follow recipes. Founder and CEO Timo Boldt markets his company on LinkedIn as 'a data company that loves food'.[26] This is a top-down message that 'we are data'.

These are no longer just digital native organisations but 'data native'. Data is at the heart of what they do and at the core of their product. In many cases, data is the product. The customer experience is enhanced with data. Improvements in operational efficiency are made with data. The data they have about us as consumers is used to drive our engagement with their services and their brand. They optimise their business and performance with data. Data and insight aren't reserved for a few people in data teams, they are baked into the fabric of the company. Decisions are routinely made with data. They have reached the 'absorbed' data pervasiveness stage.

---

26 Timo Boldt profile, https://uk.linkedin.com/in/timo-boldt

The final stage

The Optimise stage of the Level Up Framework is about reaching this panacea. It is reserved for the few but you can get there. Organisations that start life as digital and data native get there quickly. You may see elements of this happening throughout the journey but at this stage it is fully absorbed. We are optimising everything in the business through the use of data. There is no end state of this stage. The key is to keep your organisation growing, maturing, fighting and ensuring you don't see decline. Organisations that reach here tend to have innovation at their core and a mindset of continual improvements and marginal gains.

Being at this stage doesn't mean you are perfect by a long stretch. You might still make mistakes, make the wrong decisions and have poor business performance for sustained periods. If anything, it increases the expectations your stakeholders and customers have and how much you are held to account for the way data is used.

However, more good is done by organisations who are at this stage to impact the world, society and individuals. Many positive things can come from being a data-guided organisation and one where data is absorbed into the fabric of the business, its products and services. We can put data to work on some of the world's biggest problems and challenges. We can put the smartest minds with the best data sets and change things for the better. We can create a business and societal ecosystem that exists positively, in balance and corrects itself for the benefit of all. That's our hope.

Data native story: SportPursuit

SportPursuit is a UK-based inspiration-led shopping club for deal-seeking outdoor and sports enthusiasts. It is a fast-paced scale-up that is currently adding more than a million new members a year. This is no luck or coincidence but down to a well-crafted and focused team who live and breathe the idea of being a data-guided organisation.

Co-founder and Chief Data and Marketing Officer, Victoria Walton, says that:

> 'We use data everywhere. Every single person uses data to do their job. We are truly powered by data and the information we use makes us highly attuned to our customers' wants, needs and desires and ultimately has given us our success.'

While data has been used to help grow the top line, SportPursuit has been able to do this without adding cost by applying smart insights into the things that would ordinarily drive cost in a traditional, or less data-savvy, retailer.

Data is at the heart of decisions. They use data to recruit cohorts of members, targeting their paid advertising spend at people with the potential to become high-spending customers over their lifetime. They have a model that predicts each customer's lifetime value based on the first three days' worth of interactions with SportPursuit. They feed the forecast data into their advertisers to help deliver more of the right sort of people to SportPursuit's website.

Marketing spend is focused only on recruiting new members. Proprietary personalised CRM is then used to deliver long-term engagement from existing members, who continue to spend year after year, therefore delivering best in class Customer Acquisition Cost (CAC) Lifetime Value (LTV).

They also use data to help determine their ranging and choice between their diverse stock models they have set up to ensure they are only buying products they know will sell based on the knowledge they have of their customer base. Victoria explains that 'the way we choose to buy is data-driven – understanding what has worked historically and what will deliver what our customers want. That knowledge comes from not only transactions but also purchase intent by customers and customers like them.'

SportPursuit has mastered the art of using data to guide decisions by applying human smarts in setting assumptions and using experience to tweak logic.

This is done at an executive level; the senior team look at models, adjust how they work, monitor cohorts of customers and assess whether they are behaving as expected (based on data) and make strategic and operational decisions based on what they see and hear.

Some of the core models they use today were built in the very first months of the business being set up. This hasn't been retrofitted – Victoria says:

'It's been baked into the core fabric of the business from day one. It means we can hold ourselves to account, avoid lying to ourselves, avoid hiding from the bad news and focus on the granular KPIs in order to make better and sound decisions. Daily.'

New joiners in the business are tested for their data savviness and how they think and learn, as they are critical components to the culture of the organisation.

SportPursuit is a perfect example of an organisation operating at the Optimise stage of the Level Up Framework. Data is in the DNA of the business, a core part of how it operates. It is a data and digital native business growing because of the data it has and the way it is used.[27]

---

27 Interview with Victoria Walton, 21 December 2020

Data native story: Gousto

Gousto is a British meal kit retailer that supplies subscribers with recipe kit boxes which include ready-measured, fresh ingredients along with easy-to-follow recipes. It was founded in June 2012 and is now serving six million monthly meal orders. At the time of writing, Gousto has achieved 'tech unicorn' status, meaning the business is valued at over $1billion, following a recent investment round.

In order to become the nation's favourite way to eat dinner, Gousto needs to be able to provide the right level of choice to customers and create a customer experience that drives repeat use and subscription to their service. But, while Gousto is in the business of food, their founder and CEO Timo Boldt talks openly about actually being a data company that loves food. They wouldn't be able to do what they do, and grow as they have, without the innovative use of technology and data. Using data, and particularly artificial intelligence, is central to their business strategy.

This has been at the heart of the business and culture since the start of their journey. Boldt states: 'Data has been part of our DNA since day one.' They know, have experienced and continue to see the importance of data. This manifests itself culturally across the organisation in two ways. First, the company has developed and makes extensive use of data products that are built and used in order to enhance the impact on the success of their products and, importantly, the end customer experience. Second, there is a strong emphasis on using rich information to guide their decision-making, and culturally there is more than just acceptance of that but an expectation that decision-making is backed with strong evidence.

Culturally, Gousto is a data first company. They hired data scientists early in their history, and have made extensive use of data science to accelerate their growth over time. They put data at the core of what they do and this mentality is felt across the business as much as at a leadership level. They have a strong appetite to optimise their products, their supply chain and the customer experience. The business looks to proactively identify problems to solve and collaborates closely with data scientists and engineers to apply data to those problems to rapidly test and solve issues.

Gousto uses data across their operation from creating a truly personalised service, from providing targeted and relevant recipe recommendations and forecasting likely demand to optimising the route that products take around their factory and out the door to customers.

For example, Gousto is proud of its focus on giving customers variety each week in terms of the choice of menu. The company makes use of a 'data-driven menu' algorithm which optimises the recipes to display in a given week.

Within their supply chain, Gousto applies algorithms to drive operational efficiencies by optimising the routing of orders within its factories. Gousto has built data products to optimise the placement of ingredients in its factories, as well as the routing of orders within them, helping to increase throughput within its operation.

Gousto is also applying data science to create 'churn prediction models' that can identify customers likely to stop their subscription. From this information, marketing and customer care teams can react with relevant interventions through communications, offers and other means so that over time the customer interactions will become ever more personalised to focus on these customers.

Robert Barham, Gousto's Director of Data, emphasises that Gousto thinks long term about the data capabilities it needs to develop. 'Our starting point is our overall ambition several years out, and we work back from that to determine the data products we need to develop as well as the foundations that must be in place for them to be successful.' This helps them deliver for today but also build the kind of leading edge data capability that enables them to continue to grow, act and behave the way they have by applying data to every decision they make.

They make excellent use of cross-functional teams across the business to ensure they have effective business, data and technology experience solving every challenge. Barham says 'the tribe model means we have clear domain boundaries as well as close collaboration between data scientists and other technical professionals – this helps us build products quickly and with maximum impact on our end customer.'

This is a business that has started with data at its core. They put learning and continuous improvement at the heart of what they do and data forms a big part of their ability to learn and build a strong scalable business. Gousto's ambition in this space is infectious and they're a fantastic example of what it looks and feels like to be at the Optimise stage of the Level Up Framework.

PART 4

DEFINING AND DELIVERING YOUR STRATEGY

While this book has frameworks you can use to develop your data strategy and work through the journey with pace, agility and certainty, we have focused more on the mindset and concepts that will allow you to achieve this. There are elements of 'how to' but we didn't intend for this to be a step-by-step guide.

This final part of the book is aimed at providing additional practical guidance on understanding where you are, defining your strategy and your journey, and on the role of the chief data officer. This section will help you plan, plot and track your journey, bringing together the advice from the rest of the book.

SEVEN

Plotting And Tracking Your Journey

Six pillars of a data strategy

At any stage of your data journey you can take a step back and ensure you have a solid approach to data in your organisation. By applying a clear and concise method to that assessment, you can articulate where you are, where you want to be and the gap that exists between those two states.

A data strategy is a framework that enables you to deliver business value through the application of data and analytics. You should define that strategy as a written artefact to help you articulate what you plan to achieve and how you will get there. This is your story, your plan and your communication tool wrapped into one.

The following six pillars bring together all the components required when writing your data strategy. Miss any one of these in your thinking, planning or execution and you will struggle to reach your full potential, limit opportunity and slow your progress.

Vision and value

Your vision should describe the important role data plays in achieving success for your organisation and the specific business value you hope to achieve by making decisions guided by data. Successful data strategies are purposeful, focused and restless in their attempt to deliver business outcomes.

This pillar also includes the articulation of what you are solving. By aligning to the business strategy, this pillar is where you identify the key pain points and opportunities (use cases) that exist in your business and through which data can be applied to improve the decision-making about those use cases.

With this articulated you can align the rest of the data strategy pillars to it and use this pillar as a way to engage, excite and generate buy-in for your strategy.

Key outputs: vision statement, use cases prioritised based on the potential business return, information requirements (and how they map to use cases).

People and culture

Making decisions guided by data is about your people and the culture of your organisation. This pillar looks at the skills needed to be successful at implementing your strategy and how best to organise them. This needs to cover data, technical, commercial, operational and management skills. It includes defining the roles and responsibilities of teams and the individuals within those teams and the education programme you may need to improve their data fluency, knowledge and capability.

This needs to be backed up by a culture of blending intuition, experience and insights. That doesn't happen by accident so in this pillar you will be defining what you can do to start changing the culture of the business. This starts with people – what they do, how they behave, their skills, the collaboration opportunities and sharing of knowledge and projects.

Key outputs: skills required, skill gaps identified, target organisational structure, culture change activities identified and articulated.

Operating model

The approach used for prioritising, defining, delivering and managing with pace and agility can make or break your ability to deliver maximum returns from data. This pillar emphasises the importance of how your teams collaborate and cooperate with others to build data products and deliver business outcomes.

This pillar should articulate which method you will use to prioritise the business outcomes to invest energy into on a BAU basis; how you allocate that work to the teams and squads you have set up; and the approach to building your data products and services to test ideas and scale the successful ones through to a live environment. It looks at how you involve the executive and/or senior leadership to keep them engaged, bought in and up to date with the status of the data strategy. It looks to embed a mechanism for measuring and monitoring progress at a macro strategy level and a micro projects and products level.

Key outputs: prioritisation framework, chosen delivery and management methodology, approach to project governance.

Technology and architecture

There are plenty of established and innovative technologies on the market. Your ability to onboard, embed and adapt your technology platform as part of your data strategy is a huge differentiator and one that can get insight to the right people and help them create a stronger business.

This pillar looks at what technology you need in order to get hold of, manage and use data effectively. It should define the technology strategy for your data tools and how that integrates with the rest of your system landscape. It should look at assessing the architecture and data management approaches that enable you to build successful data products at pace.

Key outputs: technology strategy, technology capability gaps, architecture approach.

Data management

The key outcome of data management is to have trusted, secure and well-managed data that is ready to be harnessed to make business decisions. Without this, organisations face the challenge of relying on low-quality, uncontrolled and untraceable data, which acts like a daily tax on your organisation and blocks the rest of your strategy.

This pillar identifies the work required to improve the level of trust in your data, starting with the definitions of your key business metrics, how they are calculated and who owns them. It should look at what data you have, how it's captured, how it moves through applications and who owns each data set. It should look at how you secure data physically and through strong access controls. This pillar also looks after the quality of your data and in particular how master data sets (like customer, products, assets and so on) are created and managed.

If you are in an industry that is bound by regulatory controls, this will also need to cover how you ensure that those controls are met, documented and communicated.

Key outputs: decision on policies, standards, procedures, regulatory controls, data ownership plus creation of key metric and data catalogue.

Roadmap

A vision without a plan is just an idea. Your data strategy is not complete without a clear picture of the stages you will go through to deliver business value and build the necessary capabilities. You need an agile and adaptable plan that allows you to communicate the journey and improve at pace.

This pillar is where you pull the other five pillars together into a roadmap for delivering your data products, solutions and the order you should build out the capabilities required to help you meet your objectives.

Key outputs: a single-page roadmap.

As this is strategy and planning, there is no need to answer every single question or go into huge detail. Don't be tempted to stay in strategy forever but use it as a tool to make decisions on what you need to do and in what order.

This six-pillar approach has been successfully applied in the private, public and third sectors and in organisations from start-up to scale-up, small, medium and large enterprises. It has been successfully applied in single location, single product organisations and large multidisciplined, globally distributed organisations.

To see how you score against these six pillars, try using the Data Strategy Scorecard. Through a series of questions, it will unpick how successful your strategy is and provide you with a score and some tailored recommendations on where to focus your attention. Visit **http://datastrategyscorecard.cynozure.com** to take the test.

Relationship between data, information and business strategy

Part of the 'vision and value' pillar is about understanding the information your organisation needs. The delivery of information will be based on specific use cases and will be designed to support flexibility while driving cost efficiency, transparency and speed of delivery that meet internal and external demands.

The information you need is built from the data you consolidate for different purposes. There are three types of data set you'll need to create:

1. 10 × 10 data sets: used for published and standardised reporting.

2. 10 × 50 data sets: used for more detailed analysis and created to solve business problems or for more complex analysis and decisions.

3. 50 × 50 data sets: used for training analytical models and building decision-focused models.

These data sets should be prioritised based on the information needs of your organisation, which should be determined according to your business strategy. This ensures alignment of what your organisation is trying to achieve and how (business strategy) with the information required and business questions you need to answer (information strategy), and the data required to answer those questions.

The relationship between business strategy, information needs and data should be understood and defined and you will need to do this in a way that drives simplicity in the way you capture, store and use data. If we get this right, it allows us to shape a data ecosystem and platforms that mean you can deliver information based on the increasing complexity and range of data required against the following domains:

- **Core business reporting:** answers your business questions, serves up agreed metrics and meets any regulatory reporting you are required to do.

- **Advanced analytics:** provides outputs of models and algorithms that aim to solve business problems and deliver on opportunities through foresight and predictions. These will be iterated through 'analytics innovation' and may generate new metrics that feed into 'core business reporting'.

- **Analytics innovation:** explores new insights, metrics and predictions that are often experimental or one-off analysis. This information may or may not be published and may require ad hoc hierarchies and structures to be put in place.

- **Real-time analytics:** provides real-time operational information to run what will have become BAU activity in your organisation.

Each of these domains has a different set of characteristics about the data, how it's managed and the need for agility. The table below summarises those differences.

Domain	Veracity	Velocity	Volume	Variety	Mgmt	Agility
Core business reporting	High	Low	High	Low	High	Low
Advanced analytics	Low/mid	Mid/high	Mid/high	Mid/high	Low	High
Analytics innovation	Low/mid	Low/mid	Low/mid	Mid/high	Low	High
Real-time analytics	High	Very high	Low	Low/mid	High	High

Putting your data strategy together

At any stage of the Level Up Framework, you can take a step back and review your strategy to see whether it's still fit for purpose. Some of the pillars may need more of a focus than others but it is important to keep a close eye on all six to make sure your strategy is working for you. The difference comes from how much work there will be to (a) define your strategy and (b) implement the changes. This is all impacted by the external environment, changes in data leadership, changes in business strategy that will impact on your data strategy, and technology improvements in the market.

There are three main questions you are looking to answer in defining your data strategy:

1. What do you need to achieve against each of the six pillars (desired outcomes)?

2. Where are you today against each of the pillars (current state)?

3. How will you close the gap between the desired outcomes and the current state (activities)?

There is a tendency to focus on point two, the current state. This is often called a maturity assessment, capability assessment or health check. We don't advocate doing this as a stand-alone review because it doesn't give you a full picture. There is an element of 'so what?' about it. What your organisation really needs to know is: what will we do about it? What will we change? How will we get better and how will it impact our business?

It is best to approach this as a single set of activities to help you answer these questions in one efficient exercise that focuses on extracting maximum value from each interaction you have with your stakeholders. You will want to gather information from a cross-section of your organisation on its current ability to deliver value from data, the capabilities that exist and most importantly the business strategy you are trying to align the data strategy with. Be focused on what you are trying to achieve and know the purpose of conversations. It's easy to overload people with interviews and workshops about similar and overlapping topics and it's best to be empathetic and sensitive to people's time.

We also suggest running workshops with a cross-section of business stakeholders to identify the use cases required to deliver the business strategy, the size of the opportunity and the business questions that you would need to answer to plan for and deliver each of those use cases. These form the basis of the 'vision and value' pillar but are supplemented with the findings from the information-gathering stage.

You can then use your experience, data and judgement to articulate answers to those three key strategy questions. This book can help shape some of the approaches and options you have against those pillars. It's also important to lay out the short-term opportunities that you can crack on with, often referred to as 'quick wins' or 'low hanging fruit', as they pose an opportunity to start making a mark quickly. Be careful not to get drawn into only ever doing quick wins as this can become tactical. Make sure they contribute to the direction of travel you are outlining in the data strategy. Try to make conscious and communicated decisions rather than sleep-walking into new challenges that you'll need to clear up later.

We have seen organisations invest vast sums of money and months and months on an exercise like this. It doesn't need to be that way. For small and medium-sized organisations this should take between one and two months. For large organisations, possibly two and three months. This requires the right level of skill, experience and ability to cut through the noise and get to the point quickly.

Plotting the journey and building the roadmap

Once we've articulated the desired outcomes, the current state and the activities we need to put in place to close gaps, we are in a strong position to turn this into a plan for how the data strategy will be implemented and evolve over time. This is the sixth pillar of the data strategy, your roadmap.

The roadmap will be used to outline your expectations on when activities across the data strategy will be carried out and the order in which you will focus on the business use cases.

The roadmap isn't a fixed plan to be followed with precision but more a guide and expectation management tool. It provides important context for how the activities relate to each other and is realistic in its delivery of those activities. It needs to be responsive and adaptable to what happens as you progress and as the business evolves.

Take the full set of use cases and activities required under the data strategy pillars that you have defined and apply some prioritisation to ensure the most important and feasible things are worked on first and the dependencies between the activities. Once that is understood you can express them as initiatives in a timeline – this is your roadmap. The diagram below shows a simple and high-level one-page roadmap.

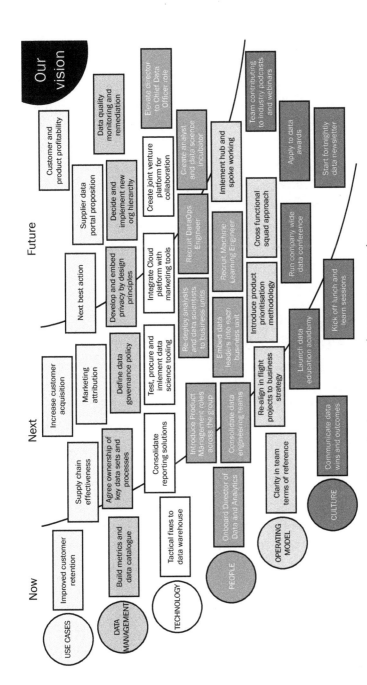

Example plan on a page data strategy roadmap

The planning horizon is down to you and should take into account budgeting cycles, visibility needs and aspiration. The tints in the roadmap can be used to indicate which pillar that activity is associated with – this often helps to show the breadth of work required.

You can use this to easily and simply communicate the 'how' of your data strategy. This shows the important steps required to achieve your vision. For stakeholders who would benefit from seeing a summary of the plan without all the associated detail, this tool works well.

The Level Up Framework as a planning tool

The beauty of the Level Up Framework is that it can act as a tool, not only to ensure you have covered what's needed in each stage of your journey but also as a way of planning the implementation of your data strategy.

By using the guidance in this book and particularly the breakthrough criteria at the end of each stage, you can build a robust plan of what you will do, when you will do it and how long you expect things to take. You can map and align your activities against the stage you are at. You can then be clear on what outcomes you are expecting at each stage and mini milestones along the way.

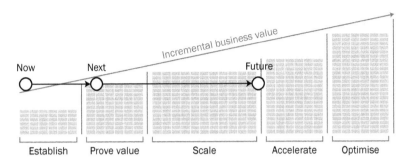

Level Up Framework states aligned to roadmap

You can use the language of this Level Up Framework day to day, to help articulate where you are and what's next. We have heard organisations say, 'We are establishing the agenda at the moment to get early investment to go and prove value,' or 'We are currently in Prove Value so the focus is on building credibility and minimum viable data products before we increase investment to scale this up.' This language helps psychologically to align the work you are doing to the stage you are at and the end point you are trying to achieve.

Measure and monitor progress

In the same way that this book talks about using data to get insight about your organisation and its performance and to ultimately guide decisions, you should also be putting in place an approach to measure, monitor and communicate the progress of your data strategy and your Level Up journey.

233

Why do we need to measure?

You have probably lost count of the number of times you have been asked, 'How is the data strategy going?' or questions to that effect. Before you know it, the answers 'Yes, not bad,' 'Getting there,' or 'Coming along!' are pouring out. Partly it depends on who is asking, the context and how formal the question is, but it is essential for the good of your strategy that you are able to articulate how it is performing in ways people can understand.

We are looking to understand whether we achieved what we set out to achieve (the outcomes), if we achieved it how we said we would (the approach) and the resources it took (time and cost). With regular retrospective reviews you can assess these questions and make decisions about changes you might need to make to your strategy and/or roadmap. These could result in short-term tweaks or longer-term adjustments but without proper assessment, measurement and data, it's difficult to make those decisions.

The act of measurement drives action. It raises accountability to the plan and commitments that have been made as part of a strategy or roadmap. Being involved with the measurement and seeing results drives increased transparency and communication, resulting in an increase in performance as everyone strives to improve outcomes. This measurement, done right, can get everyone rooting for success and aiming for a common goal that you can be proud of.

What do we need to measure?

A good measurement is one that supports the understanding needed to answer the question of how good or bad something is. It needs to encourage behaviours that have a positive effect on individuals, teams and the organisation. For that to happen the measures need to be simple to compile, clear and easy to understand. Each measure needs to be owned by someone so we know who has the responsibility to improve it.

In the case of data strategy we really should be looking to measure the following key metrics of success:

- Business outcomes of the data strategy
- Business outcomes of each data product put into action
- Costs incurred to deliver those outcomes
- Time taken to deliver those outcomes
- Throughput of data products and data product changes

In smaller organisations, where you have a clearer line of sight between activities and outcomes, this is more straightforward than a global team with siloed business units that have autonomy. Whatever your situation, there is huge benefit in a culture of capturing, measuring and communicating this in aggregate so you can ensure you are delivering value but also learning and adapting as you go.

Communicate and iterate

Communication and continual learning are at the heart of everything we have discussed in this book and form the basis of a strong data-guided culture. We should communicate and celebrate success and failure. Whatever happens, we have learned something and, if we have implemented the start-up mentality of starting small and growing the successes, we will have given ourselves a fighting chance of communicating successes more regularly. Communication is key. Transparency is vital to creating open and honest dialogue internally. Sometimes this will be uncomfortable but it allows you to move forward.

Refer back to your stakeholder map and create targeted segments of your audience to communicate to. Tailor that communication to suit the audience and pick the most appropriate medium to engage them. Some will be better in a one-to-one discussion, some prefer a report, some will need a team presentation. All of this helps with buy-in, clarity and collaboration.

A successful idea we have seen is to have an equivalent of the Golden Globes for your data strategy. How about the 'best use of data' award? The 'best improvement in query time' award? The 'best algorithm' award? The 'best newcomer' award? This less formal way of measuring success can help to engage your organisation and recognises great work and outcomes.

If you put communication at the heart of your strategy for planning, tracking and monitoring success, it will return in spades.

The modern chief data officer

When the CDO role hit the market it was heralded as a must-have. The role has grown substantially but what has not improved is clarity about what a CDO is responsible for. The CDO role is still immature and is hampered by the continual hype around data. Many executives and people in organisations know they need to care about data. However, they have also seen multiple failed data programs, the creation of data stewards and other traditional data program outcomes, which effectively make data another silo. From our personal experience as CDOs and conversations with others, here are a number of key lessons about the role.

When is a CDO not a CDO? When they are a head of data science, head of data and analytics or head of data governance. This list goes on and is a result of many organisations wanting to say they have a CDO but not really wanting to change. They want to look forward-thinking by having a CDO or data science team but don't want the cultural change needed to build a data ecosystem that can be scaled and optimised. We see a CDO as a business role, accountable on a 100% committed basis for the data strategy and value extraction, driving enablement across the organisation and leadership.

This is leadership for the development of people and for ensuring that a culture of utilising data is developed and matures over time. Leadership for the development of data products and services and ensuring strategy is aligned to business objectives. Leadership for breaking down silos and implementing a new way of working, utilising the necessary techniques like lean, Six Sigma, agile and most importantly common sense. This is a big ask. Having a technical understanding of data and the supporting technology is fundamental, but without good communication, resilience and a steely determination that data is the conduit to changing an organisation the role becomes transactional.

If you think about board level positions, they all have strategic responsibility and ensure that operational efficiency is executed correctly. They are all business roles and are likely to have input with regulators and other third parties who form part of your broader ecosystem. The CDO, therefore, should be the same. A CDO is a key role if you are to mature and scale the data products and services necessary. But does everyone need a CDO from the start? Have you ever tried pushing something twice your body weight up a steep hill? Without someone to help it is almost impossible. Whatever the size of your organisation, when you are ready to make the transition and establish the data agenda you will need help. The idea is to test and learn. Get a CDO who understands both strategically and operationally what's needed. Make them accountable for driving the data agenda. This includes aligning the strategy but also running and executing the MVPs to determine what your organisation needs to change. It requires establishing the roadmap and creating a plan for people, technology and change with the other leaders in your organisation, so it is a collaborative effort. If it is seen as a land-grab then you need to adapt and change the narrative.

As you successfully move through the stages of the Level Up Framework you will find that you bounce between the stages as you iterate and develop new products and services. Getting an organisation to change the way it operates is not a linear process, hence why we have emphasised the ecosystem complexity. At some point during the transition towards being data-guided, it is worth thinking about evolving the type of CDO you have and considering evolution and succession based on where you are on the journey and priority focus.

If a CDO understands the business, has helped to manage and understand the operations, risk, technology and data as an ecosystem that is connected, then as you plan your organisational people trajectory it is worth thinking about how you create the increased understanding of data across your key leadership roles. This could mean your CFO becoming a CDO. Whatever the outcome, having a single leadership for data is critical. It may also mean in your 'keep the lights on' structure the CDO responsibilities are consumed by another C-level role. If the organisation has evolved, this should not mean the key responsibilities discussed above are less important.

If you are developing your CDO from your C-suite, or team one level down from this, then make sure they have the aptitude to understand all the components of the role. Just as you can learn the risk frameworks, you can learn about the technology and data. The technology is moving fast and there is not a static way to manage and connect your data. Your next CDO should be adaptable, resilient and good at connecting and understanding problems. They should think about data in terms of what the organisation wants to do with it – the products and services lens we have emphasised. As in any role, if you bring someone in to create momentum for change, they need to be the right fit; if they are an existing employee make sure they are a disruptor.

A word of warning: having a token CDO is like having a paper cut-out person help you push the object up the steep hill. They need to have teeth, backing and influence. Let's look at the key capabilities and behaviours to look for in a CDO.

- **Strong business background:** the role of the CDO is a business role so the individual should be able to understand, communicate and challenge the customer. We don't see industry experience as critical – in fact it is often useful to have someone come into this role with a diverse viewpoint.

- **Negotiator and communicator:** being able to talk the language of IT, marketing, sales, finance, risk, HR and so on is critical to ensuring you can gain credibility. You will also have to highlight the awkward idiosyncrasies of the organisation; how you do that can be fundamental to people understanding why things need to change. You will need to disagree, challenge and disrupt. Being able to do this without destroying relationships is critical.

- **Understands technology:** regardless of what responsibilities you have for the infrastructure, you need to understand how it works. As a CDO it is your job to challenge the experts in your team and in IT to deliver the right architecture. The most effective method is to apply common sense. This does not mean you need to be a deep expert.

You need to be able to learn fast and apply your understanding to get the optimal solution.

- **Collaborative and adaptive:** if you are to build an approach that breaks down barriers and silos, then improving collaboration is important. This means being able to understand when you or your team need to take a backseat for the benefit of the organisation. The best ideas come when adapting to a challenge creates the spark to think differently. The outcome should always be improving the organisation.

- **Leadership:** building the right team and getting them to support and challenge the approach you are taking is key. You need to be able to draw on their expertise and have them challenge you to drive the right solution. It is your job to develop the individuals in your team. It is your job to give data a seat at the table, but not as a zero sum game. As a leader you need the organisation to follow the path you outline to create the links in your ecosystem, supporting your business objectives.

- **Listens and is pragmatic:** never assume that someone is telling you the reason they don't want to do something. It is essential to continually question and fully understand issues. Being able to do a 180° turn and still move broadly in the right direction is often how you achieve an objective. If everything were linear, the path to success would be simple.

Given the increasing importance of being digital and adaptable, especially in a COVID world (vaccine or no vaccine), there is an obvious question. Where does a successful CDO go? Do they stay as a CDO? Given the value of data to improving the operations then they could take the seat of the Chief Operating Officer or Chief Revenue Officer? If they have a finance background and the necessary qualifications, then there is no reason they couldn't become a Chief Finance Officer. For some there is definitely a path to becoming the next generation data-guided Chief Executive. If you are a CDO, this is certainly something to consider and if you have one on your board, executive team or leadership team then their progression could be a game changer for your organisation.

Reality check and looking forward

While we've shown the stages of the Level Up Framework as a step-by-step journey, it doesn't always turn out like this. People change, the environment changes, business strategy changes, technology moves on and what you think will work doesn't. You will probably take as many steps back as you do forward, need to change direction, start again, pivot and adjust. That's the point – it's about adaptability and building a culture and framework that allow (and celebrate) those things.

As things are never perfect and many aren't starting from a blank sheet of paper, some capabilities will be more advanced or behind than others. You could be at multiple stages of the Level Up Framework at once. Some parts of the data strategy may work better than others and be more progressed. This isn't a problem but you should use the framework to bring everything in line.

You will need to revisit your data strategy multiple times to refresh it, re-communicate it and pivot it around change. You can use the guidance on building and refreshing a data strategy to check you have all your stages of improvement mapped out.

It's important that you can work with ambiguity. You won't have all the answers all the time. You will need to be an adaptable leader, play up the influence skills, expect change and act as a change agent within your organisation.

Dealing with legacy

We wrote this book to push an agenda that ignores the trendy metaphors; for business people to understand that operating in silos, blaming IT and thinking data is a silver bullet for your organisational issues won't work. While we 100% believe that this approach is a winner, in reality it is only an 80% solution. Just as a great data scientist is needed to move from a correlated relationship to a causal relationship, good leadership is needed to move any organisation forward with this much change. Fix forward (see below) is a way to prioritise and make progress manageable, you will at some point need to manage the legacy.

Legacy is one of the biggest issues management faces. Keeping existing infrastructure running costs is not practical when most organisations need to reduce the expense line. Remember that this approach is not looking to create massive projects to turn off your legacy. It is based around building the right products and services to understand and manage your data. This is fundamental to the eventual decommissioning of your legacy. Unless you know what you have in your systems and what it means then any project to move to a new platform can create a program that is too big to succeed. It may sound easier just to move 'as is' but all you are doing is delaying the problem and creating a mess in your new platforms.

By focusing on building your appreciation of your data you are also building an understanding of the system infrastructure, your processes and people – not as separate components but in a more connected and transparent way. This will have an impact on how you operate and needs to be considered when you start. Too often executives think they can just fix their BI (business intelligence) team or reporting. Your data is a fundamental part of your overall ecosystem; tweaking one component may produce a result but it is unlikely to be the right result. You should now understand that data needs to be seen as a major change but can be undertaken incrementally depending on your ability to change. It can reside alongside your change activity but should be an active component. Your BAU can be managed and documented to assist the change. By the time you get to the Accelerate or Optimise stages you should have the people, infrastructure and culture to adapt, innovate and manage your ecosystems holistically.

The ecosystems you operate within are not linear, hence why the complexity is exponentially magnified. You may never need to get to Accelerate or Optimise for some services or products. The size of your organisation and the complexity of your business model and markets you operate within are always changing. It is important that tools and approaches always consider the nonlinear nature of what is being done. The ability to apply a focused approach to building people, process and products and services to support data needs to be constantly reviewed and adjusted as necessary. This does not mean changing direction when things get difficult. In too many organisations we have seen data deprioritised or management lose interest. This is because results are not being delivered or funding is reduced. It's important to have a consistent approach to understanding what needs to be done, the dependencies and your 'keep the lights on' position.

The change you are about to embark on is difficult and will be unsettling to many in your organisation. A realistic view is needed of how long and how hard it will be. Progress can be made quickly but the external ecosystem, your internal cashflow and other variables can make it slower and harder than it may first appear. It is fundamental to ensure you build the right way and bring on board people as you progress. We have provided you with several tools. All of these can be used straight out of the box or adapted to suit your organisation's idiosyncrasies.

It is essential you are ready as a leadership team to drive the change needed. You may not want to be the next Amazon but regardless of your organisation's size and ambitions we are sure you don't want to be the next Blockbuster or Kodak. There is huge potential from managing and understanding data but it cannot be treated like another silo. It needs to become everyone's responsibility. Collaboration and sharing are key facets of our approach. We can learn from others but wholly adopting best practice does not recognise that each business is different and as such we need to look at what and how we operate to create the right change.

Let's talk about a really important concept in implementing data. Every organisation is going to have legacy systems and legacy process. It is highly likely that due to the structure there will be some disconnected processes and business units operating in silos. This is the opposite of what we are trying to create. Start-up thinking, a consistent approach to data management and the Level Up Framework are there to stop this behaviour and connect the organisation. Even new organisations are likely to have some legacy. This is due, in part, to not implementing good data management up front.

If you do not change anything you will continue to create more legacy and make the problem bigger and more complex. This is where we use fix forward.

Fix forward to unshackle the past

Effectively fixing forward sees you draw a line in the sand. Fix forward is about setting a new mandate. It establishes an edict that you are going to manage process, systems, data and behaviour differently. This change recognises it is necessary for you to create an optimised data ecosystem that enables value for customers, shareholders, employees and regulators.

Fix forward is the start of your trek in using data to enable your organisational objectives. It helps you prioritise what you start on. By acknowledging you have a legacy issue and you need to change, you can scope the change. The next step will target an improvement to a BAU process or as part of an existing or new change initiative. You have not forgotten your legacy. Remember, fix forward is about that clear line and edict that things are going to be done differently. But how?

Part of the toolkit is having a clear set of data standards. Data standards form part of the consistent data management approach and are a reference point for decision-making. We all know that policy and standards do not always translate into change. You will be surprised how quickly fix forward spreads in an organisation; its power is in saying: 'I am not going to fix everything, just the new thing I am doing.' Fix forward is also pragmatic in its application. You are not trying to achieve 100% compliance with data standards. You are looking to ensure that you adopt as quickly as possible new ways of working and reduce future legacy issues being created. How quickly you progress to align to the data standards will depend on the complexity of your organisation's legacy and the current culture.

The first and most obvious place to implement fix forward is in your change portfolio. This is often the place where bad behaviours exist. At this point we recommend a chief data officer health check. If you don't have a CDO it doesn't matter. You need someone who is prepared to disrupt the change culture and challenge things using the standards. It must be a pragmatic review.

How many times have you heard a project manager say, 'Data is out of scope'? This must be one of the stupidest statements that can be made, although if there are no data standards and no understanding of what is needed from data then it is understandable. Data is pervasive across an organisation. Fix forward helps you start afresh.

Having a policy and standards only goes some of the way; the key is being able to make a review based on the necessary data products and services that data will support. It's about stopping the 'data' conversation, which is almost esoteric in nature and easy to side-step, and starting to talk about data outcomes – things you need from data. Examples include a data quality service, reference data service or lineage service; some data products include management reporting or a machine learning model accessed via a user-friendly app. Having a part of the solution is not good enough. That is why we provide a set of tools to allow you to understand what you need, when you need it and at what scale.

Neil Clutterbuck, Chief Underwriting Officer at Allianz Insurance Plc, summarises their journey:

> 'Like many organisations we had tried to get
> our data estate in order – we recognised this was
> strategically important to us and that we were
> and continue to be a data rich organisation. We
> had invested in data, but our ability to derive the
> desired returns was proving a challenge, as too
> was co-ordinating activity across federated data

teams. Our challenge was how to coordinate and extract value from our data ecosystem.

After a couple of attempts to move ourselves forward we decided to try and tackle the problem differently and appointed a chief data officer. With a CDO on board we developed a plan to create the paradigm shift that we sought. The plan was comprehensive, covering not only the what and the how, but also the cultural shift needed. Delivering against that plan was not without its issues and was hard yards. But by fixing forward and investing in understanding the products and services we needed we started to build the capabilities we needed. We invested time and effort to communicate the "how and what" we needed to change and we have progressively built and obtained value so that as an organisation we are aligned and looking to scale our capabilities. We can now exploit the value embedded in our data estate. This has been a great journey for our people and is allowing us to adapt and change at pace, just as the environment around us continues to rapidly evolve.'[28]

Fix forward is about unshackling from the past, mentally and physically. Drawing a line and giving yourself a chance of letting go and moving forward. It's easy to get busy fixing legacy; it can be a world of pain. Fix forward ensures you do not keep creating

---

28 Interview with Neil Clutterbuck, 2 December 2020

the same legacy issues and allows you to change at a pace that works for your organisation. You will need to decommission but it is important to help you do that with a sound data management foundation. It also ensures as you change, you build flexible, agile and adaptable systems in conjunction with organisation capability.

Enjoy the ride

Data really does mean business, and business really does mean data. We hope this book has helped shape your thinking, given tips for how to progress, sharpened your strategy and most of all helped to level up your organisation to adapt, evolve and scale in an ever-changing world.

Acknowledgements

Having known each other for a number of years and in conversation over a drink at an industry event, we realised that we were both considering investing time and energy into writing a book. One was a book of 'recipes' to address issues that data and business professionals encounter – with ingredients, methods and utensils to help in those situations. The other – a 'no bullshit data strategy' book – was aimed at demystifying the world of data and delivering value using a no-nonsense business-focused approach.

A whiteboard session later, we realised we both had complementary thoughts, ideas, experiences and approaches that we've seen work across a broad range of industries and organisations. This session motivated us to put pen to paper, where the basis of this book was born and over the following weeks and months, our thoughts and the story of what we wanted to say evolved into the final book we have here.

Aside from the support we have given each other through this process, we have a lifetime's worth of people we'd like to thank for helping us get here.

Jason Foster

Writing this book has been a cathartic and amazing learning experience. It's the culmination of twenty years working in a vibrant, growing and thoroughly inspiring industry. From my first boss to the latest LinkedIn connection request, every individual I engaged with is just looking to do something good in the world, and every single experience through those interactions has given me the foundations needed to put this work together.

The perfect combination of desire, motivation, time, creativity and levels of coffee required in order to write has ebbed and flowed. Much of this was written in lockdown while balancing running a business, home schooling the children, sharing workspace with the family and with the pressures of the situation ever present. I couldn't have finished this book without the help and support of so many people around me.

To my amazing wife, Victoria, for giving me time and space to think about and write this book. For listening to my updates and emotional state of mind about the writing process and giving me words of encouragement. To my children, Oliver and Alexander, for listening to me read it out loud to them (my favourite response being 'I have no idea what you just said') and showing genuine interest in the fact that Dad is writing a book. To my mum (Helen), dad (Philip), brother (Nik), sister (Tasha), brother-in-law (Gavin) and sister-in-law (Talia), for words of support and encouragement throughout.

A special thanks to Jagpal Jheeta, who has been a boss, colleague, co-founder, industry peer and friend for the best part of twenty years. Without him my company, Cynozure, would never have happened and therefore it is unlikely this book would exist.

Finally, I would like to thank the whole Cynozure crew for being such an epic and diverse team with a wonderful set of shared values and vision to help us and our customers succeed. You have all helped, directly or indirectly, this book – its cover, content, the methodologies and everything about it. We will grow, fail and succeed together. This one's for you.

Barry Green

The great thing about writing is that it gives you time to reflect on what you know. It also provides you with an opportunity to challenge your thinking, when you need to explain what you understand but can't communicate simply.

Like anything of value, it was not always easy and at times it seemed like a good idea without an end. The writing process has also created a desire to continue to challenge myself on using data better, not just for business but for everyone.

For those who have allowed me to shape and create new ideas; thank you to the Bank of Ireland, Allianz Insurance and Premium Credit, who knew they needed to change and took a chance on my approach.

A special thanks to James Cobb who sponsored my Executive EMBA, and Peter Horton and Pauline Lockett for giving me a chance to learn consulting. These two events changed my career and have allowed me to evolve. There have been too many individuals in my career who have supported me and realised there was a diamond in the rough. Thanks.

Lastly, to my partner Violina, who has endured the sleepless nights and bad moods when I could not turn off my brain. And to my son Lochlan, who was often the reason I persevered when it got tough so I could prove hard work and a good team will always produce good results.

We would like to also raise thanks to the data industry as a whole – a wonderful thriving community full of passionate and outstanding individuals, many of you trying, succeeding and evolving these methods in this book and learning together. We thank you all and hope this book does our industry justice and provides a reference material for years to come.

Of course, to the fantastic Rethink Press team who have smoothly and effortlessly helped take the book we wrote and turned it into a book that can be read. Special thanks to Kate for her time, patience, clarity and support for getting the book complete and out to the market.

Finally, we wanted to thank those who have contributed to the book directly with their stories that have ended up quoted in the book. To Phil, Jagpal, Ryan, Graeme, Pete, Anne-Claire, Neil, Victoria and Rob – thank you for trusting us with your comments to sit alongside our material. These real-world lessons are so invaluable to support our experiences and to bring everything to life. For that we thank you.

The Authors

Jason Foster is a business leader and entrepreneur. He has spent his career advising and working hands-on with organisations across the world on embedding their data into their business strategies. He cares deeply about creating a better future for all through the positive use of data and puts that at the heart of his work and his business. In 2016, Jason set up a data and analytics strategy company, Cynozure, which helps organisations to better understand and activate their data to achieve business growth and better outcomes. Jason educates and presents to thousands of data, business and technology professionals each year. He actively works to promote data leadership through his global members club, the CDO Hub, which acts as a progressive and peer-to-peer learning accelerator for chief data officers. He also hosts a podcast, Hub & Spoken, where he explores how to add value to organisations through the use of data and analytics.

🌐 www.cynozure.co.uk

🐦 @mrjasonbfoster

 **Barry Green** is a passionate chief data officer with a thirty-year career predominantly in financial services in a multitude of areas, including portfolio and relationship management, change, finance, HR, technology and re-engineering. In the CDO role, he has been building and testing his ideas on what it means to be a modern data leader. He has learned from his mistakes and loves coming up with innovative ways to solve problems. He has actively shared his leadership and ideas through international speaking engagements. Barry has also been a consultant and involved in start-ups from inception. He is an atypical data person and is convinced data is an important part of business and has real value if used to connect an organisation.

🐦 @BrG_Continuium

Lightning Source UK Ltd.
Milton Keynes UK
UKHW020827190321
380628UK00002B/51